Qualitative Method
Interpretations in
Communication Studies

Qualitative Method Interpretations in Communication Studies

James A. Schnell

LEXINGTON BOOKS
Lanham • Boulder • New York • Oxford

LEXINGTON BOOKS

Published in the United States of America
by Lexington Books
4720 Boston Way, Lanham, Maryland 20706

12 Hid's Copse Road
Cumnor Hill, Oxford OX2 9JJ, England

British Library Cataloguing in Publication Information Available

Library of Congress Cataloging-in-Publication Data

Schnell, James A., 1955–
    Qualitative method interpretations in communication studies / James A. Schnell.
        p. cm.
    Includes bibliographical references and index.
    ISBN 0-7391-0147-1 (cloth)
        1. Communication—Metholodology. 2. Communication and culture. 3.
    Communication—Study and teaching. I. Title.

P91.3 .S33 2001
302.2—dc21

00-041222

Printed in the United States of America

☉™ The paper used in this publication meets the minimum requirements of American
National Standard for Information Sciences—Permanence of Paper for Printed Library
Materials, ANSI/NISO Z39.48–1992.

This book is dedicated to Brian's grandparents—
Fred & Wanda and Li-Zhen Li & Yue-Xin Wang.

Contents

Preface

This book presents qualitative method interpretations from a communicologist perspective. Three general areas of interpretation are addressed: qualitative interpretations in cross-cultural communication, qualitative interpretation case studies, and qualitative interpretations in education (classroom and research). These interpretations are drawn from my research on communication processes. An overview of my background will provide the reader with helpful perspective on the material presented.

Most of my study has dealt with the relationship between culture and communication. A significant portion of my research has been on cross-cultural communication, most specifically focusing on the People's Republic of China. I have been to China nine times. Six of these trips were as a visiting professor at Northern Jiaotong University in Beijing.

My international travel has significantly affected my academic development. Such travel has included more than forty trips outside of the United States, to all the continents except Antarctica. Most of this travel has been as a civilian, some related to the military. I am a lieutenant colonel in the U.S. Air Intelligence Agency as a reservist. My duty has included assignments with the DIA (Defense Intelligence Agency), SOCPAC (Special Operations Command/Pacific), CINCPAC (Commander-in-Chief/Pacific), and NSA (National Security Agency).

I earned the Ph.D. at Ohio University (1982). My research has resulted in four books, more than thirty-five book chapters and journal articles and more than one hundred conference presentations. I chaired the Language and Culture Area of the American Culture Association for thirteen years and am presently a political analyst for Ohio News Network television. I have taught at rural, urban, public, and private institutions of higher education (including the University of Cincinnati, Ohio University, Miami University, and Ohio Dominican College). I have also taught in the Ohio prison system.

Part One

Qualitative Interpretations in Cross-Cultural Communication

Chapter One

The Multicultural Classroom: Working to Create Opportunities Out of Possible Obstacles

Concern with the multicultural classroom has increased considerably during the past thirty years. With more and more cultural backgrounds represented in the American classroom, it is important that faculty consider the cultural variables that are introduced in such a situation. These variables can serve as obstacles or as opportunities in the learning process. The goal of this chapter is to help faculty understand their own cross-cultural awareness in the classroom and to provide a base for improvement in this area. This goal is addressed through the use of a self-reporting instrument that faculty can use to gauge their awareness of primary areas of cross-cultural difference in the classroom. This report will not go as far as to outline right or wrong approaches, because each situation is unique.

The cross-cultural misunderstandings that occur among world cultures parallel cross-cultural misunderstandings that occur among American subcultures. Both types of misunderstandings are grounded in a lack of shared experiences and frames of reference. Sensitivity with cross-cultural differences often leads to cross-cultural awareness, which in turn leads to improved cross-cultural understanding.

Cross-cultural awareness in the multicultural classroom has become an important issue in recent years for two main reasons: a continued increase of international students studying in the United States, and an increased emphasis on faculty skills for dealing with minorities in the classroom. Regarding the latter, acts of racism have increased significantly on college campuses during recent years; minorities have responded by emphasizing the need for cross-cultural sensitivity in and out of the classroom. Unfortunately, faculty approaches to maintain cultural equilibrium in the classroom can be mistaken for cross-cultural insensitivity.

Survey 1.1, "Cultural Bound Areas for Personal Reflection," follows. These cultural bound areas are areas that can be interpreted and emphasized in significantly different ways depending upon an individual's cultural background. Thus, they can be obstacles to the learning process. The survey is based on an outline of culture bound areas that was created by the National Association of Developmental Education.

This is a self-reporting instrument. Faculty indicate their responses to each statement as: strongly agree, agree, neutral, disagree, or strongly disagree. Again, these areas are frequently interpreted and emphasized differently depending on the individual's cultural background. Awareness of these areas offers the opportunity to improve classroom interaction through greater understanding.

This survey can help faculty gauge their cross-cultural awareness by comparing and contrasting their perceptions with others who complete the survey. This instrument focuses on teacher expectations, standards, personal perspectives, approaches in common situations, and how these areas can benefit or detract from the classroom environment. Interpretation of these areas can vary depending on a persons cultural or subcultural background.

The survey addresses areas that are common bases of misunderstanding among faculty members and international students. For instance, section I, statement F states, "If a student is caught in an academically dishonest action, he/she should be expelled from school." This can be a troubling area, as what is considered "academically dishonest" in one culture can be a preferred approach in another culture. Plagiarism in the American culture is a serious offense that can result in expulsion from school. Plagiarism in China is more common since "no one owns an idea as their very own."

Awareness of these areas is also beneficial when working with the variety of subcultures that comprise U.S. culture. Misunderstandings among American subcultures are very similar to misunderstandings among international cultures. Both types of misunderstanding are based on differing frames of reference that do not necessarily indicate opposite interpretations of the culture bound areas, rather they imply various interpretations on the same continuum (but differing in varying degrees, depending on the cultural backgrounds compared).

Culture is the backdrop against which teaching and learning take place. We all use our cultural background to "filter" what we are perceiving in the classroom. Thus, the American faculty member can actually experience "culture shock" in his or her own classroom without leaving the country.

Culture shock occurs when we experience confusion, anger, or despair as a result of unsuccessful attempts to make sense of cultural practices that are foreign to us. This usually occurs when we are outside of our own culture (in another country), but it can happen when dealing with culturally different individuals in our own culture. Culture shock usually involves four stages: honeymoon, crisis, recovery, and adjustment (Schnell 1996, 150).

The honeymoon stage occurs during our initial interactions with a new culture, when we are intrigued with new places and new ways of living. The crisis stage occurs when we encounter a situation that we do not know how to resolve and we become frustrated. The recovery stage occurs when we learn how to resolve the situation. The adjustment stage occurs after we have resolved the conflict and begin to enjoy the culture again.

The aforementioned situation involving differing views on academic dishonesty between the United States and China exemplifies a culture shock situation that I experienced while teaching in China. First, I enjoyed learning new things about the Chinese culture (honeymoon). Second, I observed students plagiarizing from outside sources when writing their papers (crisis). Third, I found plagiarism is a common practice in Chinese universities (recovery). Fourth, I told my students this was against the way I had been trained in the United States but that I would adopt the Chinese approach on the issue since I was in China (adjustment).

I have experienced paralleled situations in the United States when working with culturally different students. The following four steps describe such a case. First, I had two Vietnamese students who were new to the United States. I was interested in getting to know them as I am interested in Vietnamese history and they were "boat people" who had escaped from Vietnam (honeymoon). Second, their understanding of American culture was minimal and they had great difficulty understanding various assignments in the classroom (crisis). Third, I modified their assignments, basing them on universal understandings, so they could complete the course objectives (recovery). Fourth, we achieved an academic basis for common understanding (adjustment).

Working to create opportunities out of possible obstacles in the multicultural classroom requires an appreciation of interpersonal communication. There are many rules of interpersonal interaction to consider when studying cross-cultural communication. One such model involves high and low context communication processes. In high context cultures, speakers present messages indirectly and let meanings evolve. Much is communicated through paralanguage cues and gesturing. High context cultures are located mainly in Asia (Anderson 1987, 22).

Speakers in low context cultures are more direct when presenting messages. Low context cultures are found mainly in the United States and European countries (Hall 1976; Gudykunst and Kim 1984). Awareness of these perspectives is based heavily on both verbal and nonverbal behaviors. Obviously, there is much room for confusion and incorrect interpretation of intentions.

Different perceptions of the culture-bound areas are not always a matter of differing values. Values can be similar but the expression of these values, based on cultural communicative norms, can vary significantly. Cross-cultural understanding can become especially difficult because different perceptions of culture-bound areas can be a matter of differing values *and* differing communication processes. Thus, a high degree of tolerance is beneficial in such situations.

There has been a marked increase of racism on U.S. college campuses. These situations have generally involved blatant actions exhibiting little, if any, understanding of cultural backgrounds other than dominant culture white America. Although this is a serious problem, one which could become worse before it improves, we obviously cannot focus total attention on it in our classrooms. With this issue, how we teach our classes can be more important than what we are teaching. That is, actions speak louder than words. Thus, a multicultural classroom environment that is sensitive to various cultural and subcultural backgrounds is going to help provide considerable understanding for students of all backgrounds. Obviously, the faculty member has a direct influence on this classroom environment.

It is not enough to treat culturally (or subculturally) different students like they are from your own culture (or subculture). Such a view is too ethnocentric. A basic goal can be to create a classroom environment that meets culturally different students "halfway." Intentions to establish a clear understanding can serve as a base for clear understanding. The following recommendations, general and specific, can help enhance such intentions.

Generally speaking, awareness of the affective, cognitive, and interpersonal domains of cross-cultural interaction can provide a basis for improved relations. The affective domain involves acceptance and respect of other cultural backgrounds. The cognitive domain emphasizes knowledge and understanding of other cultural backgrounds. The interpersonal domain stresses the development of communication skills for interacting with various cultural backgrounds.

In one specific approach, faculty members tape their lectures for personal review. Particular areas for evaluation include the use of sarcasm, language norms, vocal animation, supporting statements through repetition and substantiation, level of vocabulary, pronunciation and articulation, and rate of speech. All of these areas can be variables in cross-cultural interaction. Specific analysis of the following survey areas can also be beneficial.

I.   A. Teacher-student communication should be based on formal (rather than informal) interaction.
II.   A. I handle emotionally charged issues and conflict by never losing control of myself or my control over the classroom.

II. B. Humor is essential in the classroom.
III. A. It is important for me to treat students the same. They should never know if I really like them individually or not.

These areas can be evaluated using taped lectures. Again, it is important to realize these areas can vary from culture to culture. In doing this type of evaluation one should consider how one's approach fits within one's own culture/subculture and how one's approach could possibly conflict with other cultural/subcultural approaches.

Cross-cultural sensitivity (and subsequent awareness) in the multicultural classroom encourages the creation of learning opportunities out of possible obstacles. Faculty self-evaluation in this area is the first step toward understanding our weaknesses (and strengths) regarding how we can promote a better understanding of not just what we teach but how we teach it.

References

Anderson, P. A. 1987. "Explaining Intercultural Differences in Nonverbal Communication." Paper presented at the annual meeting of the Speech Communication Association (Boston) November.

Gudykunst, W. B., and Y. Y. Kim. 1984. *Communicating with Strangers: An Approach to Intercultural Communication*. New York: Random House.

Hall, E. T. 1976. *Beyond Culture*. Garden City, N.Y.: Anchor Books.

Schnell, J. A.1996. *Interpersonal Communication: Understanding and Being Understood*. East Rockaway, N.Y.: Cummings and Hathaway.

Survey 1.1

CULTURAL-BOUND AREAS FOR PERSONAL REFLECTION

SA - strongly agree, A - agree, N - neutral, D - disagree, SD - strongly disagree

I. EXPECTATIONS AND STANDARDS   SA   A   N   D   SD

    A. Teacher-student communication
       should be based on formal
       (rather than informal) interaction.

    B. Dress and cleanliness is important.

    C. If a student is academically unprepared,
       it is primarily his or her own fault.

    D. Students should have a lot of free time.

    E. Respect for authority is important.

    F. If a student is caught in an academically
       dishonest action, he or she should be
       expelled from school.

II. APPROACHES   SA   A   N   D   SD

    A. I handle emotionally charged issues
       and conflict by never losing control of
       myself or my control over the classroom.

    B. Humor is essential in the classroom.

    C. I enjoy some students less than others.

III. PREFERENCES   SA   A   N   D   SD

    A. It is important for me to treat students
       the same. They should never know if I
       really like them individually or not.

B. I prefer group (instead of individual) learning activities.

C. I prefer docile (instead of aggressive) students.

"Today we are faced with the pre-eminent fact that, if civilization is to survive, we must cultivate the science of human relationships—the ability of all peoples, of all kinds, to live together and work together, in the same world, at peace."

—Franklin D. Roosevelt, April 11, 1945

Chapter Two

Enhancement of Cross-Cultural Communication within a Multiethnic Environment: The Educational Function of the U.S. Air Force Office of Social Actions

My background is in cross-cultural communication. I am aware of ethnic and minority studies perspectives, but my academic training is not in these areas. Thus, this chapter will emphasize the enhancement of cross-cultural communication among ethnic and minority groups as exemplified through the U.S. Air Force Office of Social Actions.

Based on my military experiences, I have observed approaches practiced by the Air Force to minimize racial and sexual discrimination. They have essentially done this by incorporating federal laws into the Air Force infrastructure and exercising consistent enforcement of these policies. In this manner they are enhancing cross-cultural communication among various subcultures within the American culture.

My observations of this process have impressed me. By implementing and enforcing such policies, the Air Force minimizes racial and sexual discrimination. An individual can be promoted only by excelling according to the rules of the organization. Policies that prohibit racial and sexual discrimination are included within the rules.

This report is based on the Office of Social Actions' orientation session in which newcomers at Wright-Patterson Air Force Base are required to participate. Similar orientation sessions are presented by the Social Actions office at each Air Force base.

The beginnings of the Office of Social Actions can be traced to the Civil Rights Act of 1964. This act forbids racial discrimination in the use of publicly owned or operated facilities and in places of public accommodation. It prohibits voting registrars from applying different standards. It also forbids discrimination in employment, union membership, and federally aided programs.

By the early 1970s other indicators exemplified the need for such an office. Racial disturbances occurred at a number of military installations in a variety of geographical areas. The disturbances were perceived as growing from a lack of sensitivity, indifferent leadership, irresponsiveness on the part of supervisors, and lack of communication channels.

In more specific areas, administrative punishments were perceived as being inequitable. This perception was later substantiated statistically. For similar offenses, whites were more likely than blacks to receive counseling rather than punishment (on a scale of three to one). Also, blacks served longer pretrial confinements than whites served for the same offenses.

Government response to racial and sexual discrimination was felt in many areas of military employment. The Department of Defense (DOD) Human Goals Proclamation resulted in DOD Directive 1100.15 (The Equal Opportunity Employment Program) and DOD Directive 1322.11 (Education and Training in Human/Race Relations for Military Personnel). Civilians were also affected with the formation of Executive Order 11478, a presidential order establishing the inclusion of civilians in Equal Opportunity and Treatment (EOT) and Equal Employment Opportunity (EEO) directives.

In 1973, the Air Force established Social Actions as a career field. Air Force Regulation (AFR) 30-2 describes the career field and its objectives. AFR 30-1 clarifies Air Force standards in this area. For instance, standards of conduct require each Air Force member to treat others with respect and dignity.

AFR 30-2 outlines a variety of specific directives that are commensurate with AFR 30-1. The following list highlights representative areas of concern:

1. It is Air Force policy to conduct its affairs free of arbitrary discrimination . . . and to provide for equal opportunity for all members. . . . Commanders must take the appropriate administrative or judicial action to eliminate or neutralize discrimination and its effects.
2. Examples of unacceptable behavior are clarified. Such clarification describes that racist and sexist language, racial and ethnic humor, harassment, intimidation, and fighting are activities that violate Air Force policy.
3. Air Force members are also instructed to use a person's title or proper name (such as Mr., M., Sgt., or Capt.). First names may be used if okayed by the individual.

AFR 39-6 states that NCOs (noncommissioned officers) must actively support the Air Force human resources development programs as outlined in AFR 30-2.

Military members are all subject to the Uniform Code of Military Justice (UCMJ). The UCMJ clearly states that violations of Air Force standards, in the form of verbal and nonverbal behavior or other actions, constitute violations of, and are punishable under, the UCMJ.

As previously stated, newcomers to the Air Force are required to participate in a Social Actions orientation session. This orientation session not only describes the Air Force response to racial and sexual discrimination, but also how and why such discrimination exists and why it cannot be tolerated. Communication processes are stressed within this description. A primary premise is that individual perceptions influence interracial, interpersonal, and intercultural communication.

Communication is defined as "transmission of information, ideas, attitudes, or emotions from one person to another, by conveying those ideas through written or spoken symbols or other verbal or nonverbal signs" (Berlo 1960, 87). Perceptions and misperceptions are an important part of this process, as intended messages are not always received messages. Perceptions are defined as "information which is based on inputs from our senses and from interpretation of this data based on past and present experiences" (Smith 1966, 139). Verbal and nonverbal symbols influence interracial, interpersonal, and intercultural communication in negative and positive ways. Some of the negative effects include racist language and excluding behavior. Prejudice often exemplifies itself within these negative effects.

Prejudice is described as having three bases (Boas 1940): (1) historical—when immigrants bring "old world" prejudices with them, (2) situational—when our environment teaches us prejudice (usually due to lack of contact), and (3) character structure—individual attitudes (i.e., the less tolerant the individual the more likely prejudice will evolve or situations where individuals with frustrations have a need for a scapegoat).

The Air Force explicitly stresses that arbitrary discrimination negatively impacts on the mission and image of the Air Force. Arbitrary discrimination is broken down into six components: (1) any action, (2) unlawful or unjust, (3) that results in unequal treatment, (4) is based on age, color, national origin, race, ethnic group, religion or sex (and handicap for civilians), (5) where distinctions are not supported by legal or rational considerations, and (6) including disparaging terms or remarks (such as racist language).

Such discrimination negatively affects the individual and the mission of the Air Force in a variety of ways. For instance, an aircraft maintenance technician, who is distracted or frustrated by discrimination, may not do his or her job completely or correctly, resulting in an aircraft failure. Cases of sabotage have occurred in a variety of situations. There are many implications for this type of behavior throughout the Air Force.

The Air Force image is also important as a poor image leads to weak public confidence in the ability and functioning of the Air Force. Thus, enforcement of

Social Actions principles carries over to the local or off-base community as well. Businesses and organizations that violate EOT/EEO standards are placed off-limits to military personnel. The secretary of defense, for example, has banned members of the U.S. armed forces from active membership in racist organizations such as the Ku Klux Klan and American Nazi groups.

The recognition of differences, according to the Social Actions position, is fine. It is what we do with the recognition that determines the goodness or badness. A "Salad Bowl" approach is emphasized whereby we acknowledge individual characteristics and have an appreciation for cultural differences. As with a salad, you have a mixture of many things, each different, but adding to the flavor of the entire salad.

Air Force members are encouraged to recognize when standards are not met and to communicate policies to those who are in violation of Air Force standards. Members may seek to correct such violations by referring to the chain of command, legal office, inspector general, chaplain, or Social Actions office. Civilian employees also have an EEO representative. Corrective actions for violations include verbal or written counseling, letter of reprimand, Unfavorable Information File/Control Roster, Article 15, APR/OER (airman performance report/officer effectiveness report) comments, removal from supervisory position, separation from the service, or court-martial.

Social Actions regulations will not completely stop racial and sexual discrimination. But their enforcement can clearly be interpreted as a thorough benefit to cross-cultural communication within a multiethnic environment such as the U.S. Air Force.

References

Berlo, D. K. 1960. *The Process of Communication*. New York: Holt, Rinehart, and Winston.

Boas, V. 1940. *Language, Race and Culture*. New York: Macmillan.

Smith, A. G., ed. 1966. *Communication and Culture*. New York: Holt, Rinehart, and Winston.

Chapter Three

Cross-Cultural Toleration and Its Effect on Classroom Communication in South African Universities: A Survey of South African Faculty Members

The February 11, 1990, release of Nelson Mandela marked another step in the antiapartheid reforms implemented in South Africa. Antiapartheid reforms have been sought in practically all areas of South African life, including economic, political, and educational reforms. This chapter will focus on the current classroom situation in South African universities and how cross-cultural toleration can affect classroom communication. This analysis is intended to serve as an indicator of educational shortcomings, regarding cross-cultural communication in the classroom, and establish a need for modifications in this area. Before focusing on education in South Africa, a brief overview of the country will provide helpful context for the current situation.

South Africa and Apartheid

South Africa is roughly three times the size of California. Seventy-five percent of its population (36 million) is black, 14 percent white, 8 percent coloreds (mixed black/white/Asian), and 3 percent Asian and others. Race relations are controversial and much of the present controversy stems from apartheid. Apartheid, a Boer word meaning separate, is a policy that provides for legalized compulsory separation of the races. This policy was instituted in 1948 when the National Party came to power. During the 1960s black rights were further reduced due to the threat posed by the African National Congress, which Mandela led (Dostert 1987, 93-98).

I visited South Africa for two weeks in July 1989 to present a workshop on cross-cultural communication in the classroom at the annual national meeting of the South African Applied Linguistics Association, held at the University of Natal in Durban. The University of Natal, at the time, was one of five universities that openly rejected apartheid.

My visit allowed for observation of day-to-day life in South Africa. In comparison to U.S. standards, I observed limited meaningful black-white interaction. Interaction between blacks and whites evidenced indifference but very little overt anger. There seemed to be a peaceful coexistence for the most part, almost as if racially different persons are to be seen but not interacted with, unless given a reason to do so. It was as if each race knew "its place" and acted accordingly.

It is difficult to comprehend how devastating intoleration between blacks and whites must be on cross-cultural communication in the classroom. Speculation on this subject is a primary concern of this chapter.

Cross-Cultural Communication

Study of cross-cultural communication has increased significantly since World War II. World trade and international exchange have helped perpetuate this increase. As the classroom becomes more culturally diverse it is important for faculty to consider the cultural variables that are introduced in such a situation. These variables can serve as obstacles or as opportunities in the learning process. Sensitivity with cross-cultural differences can lead to cross-cultural awareness, which in turn will lead to improved cross-cultural understanding. These cultural variables are obstacles to learning in South Africa.

Surveys 3.1, 3.2 and 3.3, titled Cultural Bound Areas for Personal Reflection, are included at the end of this chapter. These cultural-bound areas are areas that can be interpreted and emphasized in significantly different ways depending on an individual's cultural background. Thus, they can be obstacles to the learning process. The survey is based on an outline of culture-bound areas that was created by the National Association of Developmental Education. This is a self-reporting instrument. Faculty indicate their responses to each statement in each area: strongly agree, agree, neutral, disagree, and strongly disagree. Again, these areas are frequently interpreted and emphasized differently depending on the individual's cultural background. This instrument focuses on teacher expectations, standards, personal perspectives, approaches in common situations, and how these areas can benefit or detract from the classroom environment.

Awareness of these areas is also beneficial when working with the variety of subcultures that comprise individual cultures. Misunderstandings among subcultures are very similar to misunderstandings among international cultures. Both types of misunderstandings are based on differing frames of reference thatdo not necessarily indicate opposite interpretations of the culture bound areas; rather, they imply various interpretations on the same continuum, differing in varying degrees depending on the cultural backgrounds compared.

The effect of the cultural backgrounds of interactants on human interaction is a crucial consideration. "Culture is the enduring influence of the social environment on our behavior including our interpersonal communication behaviors" (Andersen 1987, 6). The culture of an individual dictates interpersonal behavior through "control mechanisms—plans, recipes, rules, instructions (what computer engineers call 'programs')—for the governing of behavior" (Geertz 1973, 44). Thus, the processes for presentation of ideas (speaking) and the reception of ideas (listening) will understandably vary from culture to culture.

The implications of high and low context communication processes, across cultures, provides an example of the effect of culture on the interaction process. "A high-context communication message is one in which most of the information is either in the physical context or internalized in the person, while very little is in the coded, explicit, transmitted parts of the message" (Hall 1976, 91). For instance, people who know each other very well can communicate through unexplicit messages that are not readily understandable to a third party. "In high context situations or cultures, information is integrated from the environment, the context, the situation, and from nonverbal cues that give the message meaning unavailable in the explicit verbal utterance" (Andersen 1987, 22).

Low context messages (and cultures) are just the opposite of high context messages; most of the information is in the explicit code (Hall 1976). Low context messages must be elaborated, clearly communicated, and highly specific (Andersen 1987, 22). The lowest context cultures are probably Swiss, German, North American (including the United States) and Scandanavian (Hall 1976; Gudykunst and Kim 1984). These cultures are preoccupied with specifics, details, and precise time schedules at the expense of context (Andersen 1987, 22).

The highest context cultures are found in Asia. China, Japan, and Korea are very high context cultures (Elliot, Scott, Jensen, and McDonough 1982; Hall 1976). "Languages are some of the most explicit communication systems but the Chinese language is an implicit high context system" (Andersen 1987, 23). Americans (from a low context culture) will complain that Japanese speakers (from a high context culture) never "get to the point." This is due to a failure to recognize that high context cultures must provide a context and setting and let the point evolve (Hall 1984).

People in high context cultures expect more than interactants in low context cultures (Hall 1976). Such expectations assume the other person will "understand unarticulated feelings, subtle gestures and environmental clues that people from low context cultures simply do not process. Worse, both cultural extremes fail to recognize these basic differences in behavior, communication,

and context and are quick to misattribute the causes for their behaviors"
(Andersen 1987, 25). Similar degrees of disparity on the high context-low
context continuum can exist among subcultures.

Different perceptions of the culture-bound areas are not always a matter of
differing values. Values can be similar but the expression of these values, based
on cultural communicative norms, can vary significantly. Cross-cultural understanding can become especially difficult because different perceptions of
culture-bound areas can be a matter of differing values and differing
communication processes. A high degree of tolerance is beneficial. How faculty
teach their classes can be more important with this issue than what they are
teaching. Thus, a multicultural classroom environment that is sensitive to
various cultural and subcultural backgrounds is going to help provide
considerable understanding for students of all backgrounds. Obviously, the
faculty member has a direct influence on this classroom environment.

Culture-Bound Survey Findings

I have used the aforementioned survey while leading faculty workshops,
focusing on the multicultural classroom, in the United States and South Africa.
Comparison and contrast of faculty responses to these survey areas exemplify
the void between U.S. and South African faculty perspectives. The survey was
used in March 1989 with ninety-seven English/speech/linguistics faculty
members at the annual Conference on Student Success Courses held in Orlando,
Florida. The survey was also used in July 1989 with 112 English/
speech/linguistics faculty members at the annual meeting of the South African
Applied Linguistics Association held in Durban. Neither group offers a perfect
standard to evaluate other nationalities by, but comparison and contrast do
highlight differences that exist between cultures, allowing for examination of
why they vary regarding cross-cultural perspectives.

Responses by South African faculty members are shown in Survey 3.1. The
numbers noted on the survey are percentage responses to each area. Review of
the survey responses indicates strong consistencies in most areas. For instance,
87 percent prefer formal communication rather than informal communication
with students, 78 percent consider dress and appearance as important, 89 percent
believe academic preparation is the student's responsibility, 89 percent feel
respect for authority is important, and 84 percent state cheating should result in
expulsion.

Responses given by American faculty members are in Survey 3.2. The
numbers noted on the survey are percentage responses to each area. Review of
these survey responses, in contrast with the South African responses, indicates
considerable diversity regarding faculty perspectives on the culture-

bound-areas. American society is diverse. Perhaps this cultural diversity is a base for the diverse interpretations noted in the survey. Again, it is important to remember there are no correct or incorrect responses to survey areas. The survey merely gauges respondent perspectives as they relate to cultural norms.

Survey 3.3 compares and contrasts responses by U.S. and South African respondents. As noted at the top of the survey, American majority responses are indicated with an "X" and South African majority responses are indicated with an "O". Review of these responses indicates similarities and differences between the two groups. Most notable are four areas that show radically different perspectives. These are I.A. (teacher-student communication should be formal), I.F. (cheating should result in expulsion), II.A. (importance of treating students the same), and III.C. (respect for authority).

In each of the areas where responses differ, the South African group differs in favor of faculty dominance in the classroom. South African faculty indicate teacher-student communication should be formal, student cheating should result in expulsion, it is not necessary to treat students the same, and a preference for docile students. In contrast, the American group indicates teacher-student communication should be informal, student cheating should not result in expulsion, it is necessary to treat students the same, and a preference for aggressive students. Even in areas where both groups agree, the South African group indicates stronger faculty dominance. In area I.E., 70 percent of the American respondents feel respect for authority is important compared to 89 percent of the South African respondents who feel respect for authority is important.

Conclusion

An analysis such as this stands, to a considerable degree, on the accuracy of generalizations made from survey data collected. Of the 112 South African English/speech/linguistics faculty members who completed the survey, 110 respondents were white and two were black. Thus, it is safe to make generalizations from the survey data as being representative of white South African English/speech/linguistics faculty members. As stated earlier, neither group offers a perfect standard to evaluate other nationalities by, but comparison and contrast does highlight differences that exist between cultures, allowing for examination of why they vary.

Using faculty members as an indicator, and based on the information gathered with this survey, the South African academic community exercises more dominance in the classroom. The South African faculty preference for dominance results in less tolerance of cross-cultural diversity (when compared against the U.S. academic community), because tolerance of cross-cultural diversity requires flexibility when working with diverse backgrounds, and the needed flexibility can hinder faculty dominance.

There is nothing in the survey data that describes characteristics of culturally different groups in South Africa. However, it is a safe assumption such characteristics are expressed through high context and low context communication channels. Regardless of these characteristics, or how they are communicated, the survey findings indicate South African faculty members prefer more dominance (as compared to American faculty) and this preference for dominance results in less flexibility and subsequent intolerance for cultural frames of reference different than their own.

Consideration of high and low context communication, as a variable in cross-cultural interaction, provides insight into the unique cultural climate of South Africa. The white South Africans are primarily from England. European cultures tend to interact through low context channels (Hall 1976; Gudykunst and Kim 1984). The vast majority of black South Africans are obviously from Africa and Africans are characterized as using more high context communication channels than Europeans. Thus, interaction between black and white South Africans should be interpreted in light of this difference.

One might argue that black and white South African cultural backgrounds have had a chance to fuse over the years, allowing for adaptation and familiarization, as has happened in the United States. However, apartheid has greatly reduced interaction among culturally different South Africans and this, in turn, inhibits the adaptation and familiarization process. Thus, the high context and low context communication norms used by black and white South Africans are reinforced.

Faculty members who teach English, speech, and linguistics in the United States and South Africa have been used as representative samples to generalize faculty perceptions regarding survey areas. The United States and South Africa have cultural diversity but the main difference is that South Africa has far less interaction among its culturally different populations. Integration is legislated in the United States while segregation (apartheid) is legislated in South Africa.

I contend separation among racial groups leads to ignorance about other racial groups, which leads to fear of other racial groups. A symptom of this problem in South Africa is the institution of apartheid. Alex Boraine, executive director of the Institute for a Democratic Alternative for South Africa, summarizes a similar view in the South African press: "Many white South Africans have genuine deep-rooted fears . . . the causes of such fears were largely attributable to widespread ignorance of black people. . . . Whites and blacks for the most part live in different worlds, and isolation breeds ignorance, which brings with it fear" (Boraine 1989, 3).

As long as this condition exists in South Africa the communicative climate in the classroom will likely suffer as a result of the described lack of cross-cultural toleration. Awareness can be the first step toward social change. South African faculty can promote positive social change through emphasis on cross-cultural toleration in their classrooms.

References

Andersen, P. A. 1987. "Explaining Intercultural Differences in Nonverbal Communication." Paper presented at the annual meeting of the Speech Communication Association, Boston (November).

Boraine, A. 1989. "Whites fears of the future cannot be ignored," *Natal Mercury* (7 July) 3.

Dostert, E. 1987. *The World Today Series: Africa 1987*. Washington, DC: Stryker-Post Publications.

Elliot, S., M. D. Scott, A. D. Jensen, and M. McDonough, 1982. "Perceptions of Reticence: A Cross-Cultural Investigation," in *Communication Yearbook 5*, ed. M. Burgoon. New Brunswick, NJ: Transaction Books.

Geertz, C. 1973. *The Interpretation of Cultures*. New York: Basic Books.

Gudykunst, W. B. and Y. Y. Kim, 1984. *Communicating with Strangers: An Approach to Intercultural Communication*. New York: Random House.

Hall, E. T. 1976. *Beyond Culture*. Garden City, NY: Anchor Books.

———. 1984. *The Dance of Life: The Other Dimension of Time*. Garden City, NY: Anchor Books.

Survey 3.1: South African Faculty*

CULTURAL-BOUND AREAS FOR PERSONAL REFLECTION

SA - strongly agree, A - agree, N - neutral, D - disagree, SD - strongly disagree

* The survey was answered by 112 faculty members. Numbers noted below are the percentage of responses.

I. EXPECTATIONS AND STANDARDS	SA	A	N	D	SD
A. Teacher-student communication should be based on formal (rather than informal) interaction.	16	71	4	5	4
B. Dress and cleanliness is important.	23	55	7	10	5
C. If a student is academically unprepared, it is primarily his or her own fault.	33	56	1	7	3
D. Students should have a lot of free time.	2	5	18	58	17
E. Respect for authority is important.	37	52	8	3	0
F. If a student is caught in an academically dishonest action, he or she should be expelled from school.	26	58	2	12	2

II. APPROACHES	SA	A	N	D	SD
A. I handle emotionally charged issues and conflict by never losing control of myself or my control over the classroom.	14	76	6	4	0
B. Humor is essential in the classroom.	5	50	3	33	9
C. I enjoy some students less than others.	20	44	13	17	6

III. PREFERENCES

	SA	A	N	D	SD
A. It is important for me to treat students the same. They should never know if I really like them individually or not.	12	13	6	47	22
B. I prefer group (instead of individual) learning activities.	6	6	12	58	18
C. I prefer docile (instead of aggressive) students.	7	65	8	13	7

Survey 3.2: American Faculty*

CULTURAL-BOUND AREAS FOR PERSONAL REFLECTION

SA - strongly agree, A - agree, N - neutral, D - disagree, SD - strongly disagree

* The survey was answered by 97 faculty members. Numbers noted below are the percentage of responses.

I. EXPECTATIONS AND STANDARDS	SA	A	N	D	SD
A. Teacher-student communication should be based on formal (rather than informal) interaction.	8	22	0	55	15
B. Dress and cleanliness is important.	6	23	45	15	11
C. If a student is academically unprepared, it is primarily his or her own fault.	5	44	20	25	6
D. Students should have a lot of free time.	11	30	14	43	2
E. Respect for authority is important.	11	59	23	7	0
F. If a student is caught in an academically dishonest action, he or she should be expelled from school.	9	36	11	41	3

II. APPROACHES	SA	A	N	D	SD
A. I handle emotionally charged issues and conflict by never losing control of myself or my control over the classroom.	2	81	4	13	0
B. Humor is essential in the classroom.	14	38	15	30	3
C. I enjoy some students less than others.	19	65	2	14	0

III. PREFERENCES

	SA	A	N	D	SD
A. It is important for me to treat students the same. They should never know if I really like them individually or not.	32	36	0	29	3
B. I prefer group (instead of individual) learning activities.	6	29	7	51	7
C. I prefer docile (instead of aggressive) students.	4	30	22	37	7

Survey 3.3: Comparison of American Faculty (X) and South African Faculty (O)

CULTURAL-BOUND AREAS FOR PERSONAL REFLECTION

SA - strongly agree, A - agree, N - neutral, D - disagree, SD - strongly disagree

* The survey was answered by 112 faculty members. Numbers noted below are the percentage of responses.

I. EXPECTATIONS AND STANDARDS	SA	A	N	D	SD
A. Teacher-student communication should be based on formal (rather than informal) interaction.			O	X	
B. Dress and cleanliness is important.			O	X	
C. If a student is academically unprepared, it is primarily his or her own fault.		X O			
D. Students should have a lot of free time.				X O	
E. Respect for authority is important.		X O			
F. If a student is caught in an academically dishonest action, he or she should be expelled from school.			O	X	

II. APPROACHES	SA	A	N	D	SD
A. I handle emotionally charged issues and conflict by never losing control of myself or my control over the classroom.		X O			
B. Humor is essential in the classroom.		X O			
C. I enjoy some students less than others.		X O			

III. PREFERENCES

	SA	A	N	D	SD
A. It is important for me to treat students the same. They should never know if I really like them individually or not.		X		O	
B. I prefer group (instead of individual) learning activities.				X O	
C. I prefer docile (instead of aggressive) students.			O	X	

Chapter Four

Mass Media and the Impact of International Peacekeeping, Peace-Enforcement, and Humanitarian Operations on U.S. National Security Strategy

This chapter will analyze the impact of international peacekeeping, peace-enforcement and humanitarian operations on U.S. national security strategy since 1992. This analysis will focus on the consistent relevance of mass media and the role the media play regarding such variables as political considerations, human rights, and military capabilities.

A specific point to be illustrated is that mass media affect the decision-making process related to the evolution of international peacekeeping, peace-enforcement, and humanitarian operations. An extensive review of literature has been done to procure legitimate sources that address such effects since 1992. This review has produced a broad collection of materials that consider such operations from the macro and micro levels. The former typically convey general perspectives that can be used to understand common issues; the latter address more specific applications and situations. Representative findings from the aforementioned will be used to illustrate consistent themes. Most of the materials analyzed were based on qualitative studies. This makes the findings of this chapter especially relevant in the larger context of this book.

Background

Analyzing and evaluating the use of U.S. armed forces in international peacekeeping, peace-enforcement, and humanitarian operations, in relation to U.S. national security, is a fluid proposition. That is, the primary variables and their relationship to each other are in continuous movement, much like a constellation of stars. What was relevant last year may be less relevant this year. The situation today barely resembles the situation ten years ago.

The end of the Cold War has had a tremendous impact on our national security and how we understand it. Today the United States tends to try to define its national security strategy in terms of protecting its national interests. A big challenge in this process has been to achieve consensus on what U.S. national interests are in particular situations and then decide the best approaches for protecting these interests. Oftentimes these interests are indirectly linked to the United States but, taken together, they tend to tip the balance in favor of U.S. intervention.

The concept of military operations other than war has taken on a critical significance since the end of the Cold War. The threat from the former Soviet Union has now splintered into many smaller, yet still relevant, threats in a variety of places around the world. At present, these military operations other than war have manifested themselves in such contemporary phenomena as international peacekeeping, peace-enforcement, and humanitarian operations.

Definitions for these concepts are best realized by understanding them in the context of actual situations rather than literally worded dictionary definitions without application. Minear and Guillot explain that:

> A half decade after the fall of the Berlin Wall and the breakup of the former Soviet Union, military establishments in both East and West were less seized with traditional tasks and newly available for what have come to be called operations other than war. At the same time, the increased incidence of major emergencies and a growing willingness to use troops to respond had contributed to the evolution of outside military forces as a significant actor in the humanitarian sphere. (1996, 17)

U.N. Secretary General Kofi Annan, in an analysis of peacekeeping and national sovereignty, defines peacekeeping, peace-enforcement, and humanitarian operations within the context of Somalia, the former Yugoslavia, and Rwanda. He explains humanitarian operations as working to achieve humanitarian goals through the uncommon use of military force, peacekeeping as having a mandate to disarm those with weapons and to deliver humanitarian relief, and peace-enforcement as including reconstruction objectives such as rebuilding the nation under occupation (Annan 1998, 60).

This chapter will analyze the operations in the former Yugoslavia, Somalia, and Rwanda, all of which have included U.S. military personnel. It has been imperative to build this analysis on concrete data, findings, and conclusions.

The former Yugoslavia posed a very complex situation for the United Nations. The challenges were many and the expectations exceedingly high. Participation by the international community made the Balkans a testing ground that exposed shortcomings of diplomacy and the need to use force in such situations (Leurdijk 1997, 69). "Taken together the UN's role encompassed a conceptual framework for this involvement in terms of preventive diplomacy, peace-making, peace-keeping, humanitarian assistance, peace-enforcement and subcontracting between the UN and regional organizations" (Leurdijk 1997, 71).

The primary objectives for the United Nations were to keep the conflict within Croatia, Bosnia, and Herzegovina, implement a cease-fire, establish a settlement for conflicts in the area, and undertake a large humanitarian operation. The use of the military to achieve these objectives can incorrectly link the notion of peacekeeping with using force. However, peacekeeping is not a military concept. Paradoxically, "peace-keeping is not a soldier's job, but only a soldier can do it" (Leurdijk 1997, 72). This is typical of how gray areas can become awkward contradictions.

A primary lesson from operations in Somalia is that such endeavors lack a political capability. The stages of foreign participation in Somalia built through three steps typically found in such type of operations: peacekeeping through diplomacy, peace-enforcement through the military, and attempts at peace-maintenance through political channels (Chopra and Watson 1997, 101). The latter proved to be especially problematic.

U.S. military involvement in southwest Rwanda evidenced a unique type of participation. That is, the U.S. military carried out a number of activities in the area but did so without placing humans on the ground. Such actions included overflights, transport, and reinforcement. They were successful for the most part and lent considerable stability for the cause being promoted (Minear and Guillot 1996, 114).

As noted earlier, U.S. foreign policy has been experiencing significant changes since the end of the Cold War. The debate today deals with what the United States should be doing with its influence, given the aforementioned problems, for example (Snow and Brown 1997, 25). The competing perspectives are neoisolationism, selective engagement, cooperative security, and primacy (Posen and Ross 1997, 6). These perspectives differ considerably. Worth noting is that the isolationist end of the spectrum can be extended further in the direction of noninvolvement when one sees this extreme, not just as isolationism, but disinterest (Dunn 1996, 238).

With the U.S. role in world affairs increasing in matters such as international peacekeeping, peace-enforcement, and humanitarian operations, one might understand how such involvement could be interpreted as hegemonic activity by the United States. This view is frequently trumpeted in international circles but many recognize U.S. leadership as providing necessary guidance in an unstable world (Kagan 1998, 26). This phenomena has been symptomatic of a globalization process that continues to evolve. U.S. technology, including U.S. mass media, has enhanced U.S. leadership around the globe.

During globalization the world becomes a smaller place. That is, it has become more connected. Marshall McLuhan spoke of a global village whereby inhabitants from various regions of the world are connected through electronic communications. This has worked to minimize the impact of time and space. In many respects, we can communicate with those around the world almost as easily as we can with those across town (Smith and Bayliss 1997, 8). U.S. mass media have been leading these developments. This increased connectivity has enhanced the ability of media messages to impact worldwide interpretation of events instantaneously, and significantly affect the political consequences of such interpretation. Such consequences include the degrees of international response as a result of occurrences.

Issues Analysis

This section deals with political considerations, human rights, and military capabilities regarding their impact on the decision to employ U.S. forces in international peacekeeping, peacemaking, and humanitarian operations. Analysis will consider the role mass media plays with the aforementioned variables. As clarified in the previous section, examples will be drawn from U.S. military involvement in the former Yugoslavia, Somalia, and Rwanda.

Political Considerations

A basic understanding of mass media effects is essential to grasping how political considerations impact U.S. decision making regarding whether to engage in international peacekeeping, peacemaking, and humanitarian operations. The basic understanding is also relevant with analysis of human rights and military capabilities. Mass media effects, while not always the most important factors, are common and relevant in all three areas (political considerations, human rights, and military capabilities). Political issues are considered to be more relevant in most scenarios than are human rights and military capabilities.

The previous section conveyed a cursory overview of how compression of time and space has created a global village that Marshall McLuhan described more than thirty years ago. McLuhan spoke of four periods of unique relevance in the study of communication in society. First was the preliterate, "tribal society," which stressed face-to-face interaction. Second was the "civilized detachment society" which evolved with the phonetic alphabet and manuscript technology (whereby the eye becomes more important than the ear). Third was the "Gutenberg society" which built on the phonetic system and was catapulted by the printing press. This period was especially unique because, with the ability to produce books in mass quantities, individuals could learn and store a lot of information without much interaction with others (Golden et al. 1997, 157).

The fourth (and present) period is "electronic society." McLuhan contends that electric circuitry has significantly compressed the previous limitations of time and space. It has restructured our interaction processes to include, instantaneously, others from around the world whereby we have a global village (Golden et al. 1997, 158). This is especially relevant when we analyze the impact of political considerations (human rights and military capabilities) on U.S. decision making that affect international peacekeeping, peacemaking, and humanitarian operations, because the speed with which information and images are conveyed can detract from, or override, logical decision-making processes that might otherwise be employed. Emotional images conveyed on CNN can be stronger than logical factual data affecting political considerations, the understanding of human rights issues, and interpretation of military capabilities.

On September 17, 1998, former Senator Bob Dole testified on the atrocities in Kosovo during a hearing before the Commission on Security and Cooperation in Europe. Dole accused western diplomats of avoiding a challenge to Slobodan Milosevic. He went on to clarify the political aspects of the situation in Kosovo: "The problem in Kosovo is not by definition a humanitarian one. It is a political and military crisis, whose most visible symptoms are humanitarian. And so, while more humanitarian aid is desperately needed, such assistance will not solve the problem" (Dole 1998, 38). Dole's statement made a clear assertion that the political considerations in Kosovo were strong enough to warrant a military solution to the problem. Hence, it is evidenced how political considerations are a primary determinant within a given context.

Human Rights

Human rights, as a reason to perpetuate U.S. military intervention in international peacekeeping, peacemaking, and humanitarian operations, has received a strong boost from the continued evolution of mass media. "Television coverage has had a remarkable impact upon western charity. . . . As a medium, television dramatically reduced the lag-time between pressure and action, between need and response" (Ignatieff 1997, 10). Television has helped create a new kind of politics that has built a world opinion framework that monitors the rights of those who do not have the ability to care for themselves (Ignatieff 1997, 21).

Addressing human rights concerns requires intervening nations to fully comprehend the human dimensions of a given scenario. For instance, the emotional elements of Rwanda's problems can best be understood by first grasping Rwandan history, subcultures, social divisions, and perceived injustices. This requires U.S. representatives to acknowledge and consult individuals, such as spiritual leaders, who are not typically part of the diplomatic environment (Hackett 1997, 94). Looking beyond standard diplomatic channels will no doubt be more challenging but, if that is where the answers are, then that is where the seekers must go.

Much information related to the Rwandan situation, though not necessarily all the primary information, could be seen in mass media coverage of the crisis. The new communication technologies have perpetuated positive and negative mass media effects. Some of the positive effects include: (1) a larger global public access to information sources that governments can extend little, if any, control over; (2) subcultural communities have an enhanced ability to express themselves; and (3) international newsgathering capabilities have grown. Some of the negative effects include: (1) a deterioration of quality news programming for general audiences; and (2) a lowering of journalistic standards, because improved technology has not equated with improved reporting (Giradet 1996, 46-47). Any accurate analysis of the human rights issues in Rwanda, used in decision-making processes regarding whether to employ U.S. military intervention, would be affected by these variables.

Military Capabilities

A decision to commit U.S. military troops in international peacekeeping, peacemaking, and humanitarian operations must consider U.S. military capabilities. There is little doubt the U.S. military has ample firepower to defend itself in most situations. The question typically rests with military capability to strategically employ that firepower, if it is even needed, to meet the established objectives of humanitarianism.

U.S. leaders who commit U.S. troops carry a heavy moral burden. "The surface lesson of the U.S. intervention in Somalia (1992-1995) is that any activity overseas that has indistinct or only partially articulated humanitarian political goals (and is not simply a relief effort) is immediately hostage to the loss of American lives" (Rotberg 1997, 230). There is also a ripple effect to consider in that the Clinton administration avoided military intervention in the

Rwanda genocide (April 1994) partially because of the deaths of eighteen U.S. service personnel in Somalia six months earlier (Clarke and Herbst 1997, 239).

The role of the mass media in this ripple effect clearly should not be understated. CNN and other world media conveyed graphic footage of dead U.S. service personnel being dragged through Somalian streets in front of cheering crowds. This coverage clearly posited the question "What are we doing in Somalia?" Given the lack of clearly stated military objectives, there was not much of an answer to the question. Thus, the U.S. military was much more reticent to get involved in Rwanda six months later. The immediacy of questioning U.S. involvement in Somalia would not have been nearly as strong had there not been worldwide conveyance of the abuse of dead U.S. soldiers.

Thus, the impact of military capabilities on the decision for or against U.S. military intervention should be expressed in terms of clearly stated military objectives that are achievable and measurable. "The first, and most fundamental (lesson from Bosnia), is that without clarity of aims, strength of purpose and depth of commitment, any international effort is almost certain to flounder" (McLean 1996, 15).

Policy Evaluation

U.S. policy regarding the use of U.S. military forces in peacekeeping, peace-enforcement, and humanitarian operations to meet U.S. national security strategy objectives, can be measured against the five criteria of national interests, costs, risks, military readiness, and U.S. public support. What follows are the findings from such an evaluation. This evaluation considers the importance of mass media interpretations of these criteria.

National Interests

The national interests criterion is the most significant of the five criteria. Individual nations typically participate meaningfully with foreign crises solutions only when their national interests are threatened (Dallaire 1998, 72). As such, a nation must be able to define its national interests, prioritize these national interests, and decide the best way to protect or advance them in a given situation. How the mass media, within the nation and outside the nation, conveys these interests and the situation overall will affect how the nation will define, prioritize, and promote these interests. Thus, the effect of the media in this process should not be overlooked.

Sometimes national interests assessment can be vividly clear, and at other times it will require more abstract interpretation. For instance, the end of the

Cold War has created a situation in Europe whereby the greatest threat to the security and national interests of most nations comes from economic decline and instability within a given nation rather than from foreign aggression (Tedstrom 1997, 3). Mass media interpretations will not always enhance the accuracy of such an understanding.

Therefore, it is important that a nation has the ability to clearly grasp the objectives it is seeking to achieve and how it will achieve these objectives. Political variables, as conveyed (accurately or inaccurately) via mass media, are part of this process. If the political aspect muddles along without clarification, and a strategic plan is not clearly stated, military troops will become the first casualties (Dallaire 1998, 72).

Costs

There are significant costs related to military participation in peacekeeping, peace-enforcement, and humanitarian operations. Achievement of U.S. national security strategy objectives can be greatly hindered if adequate resources are not allocated to meet these objectives. The need for such resources has increased significantly in the past ten years.

U.S. military intervention in foreign disasters has been ongoing for many years. It was a fairly simple process until the 1990s. The Office of Foreign Disaster Assistance contracted U.S. military aircraft to haul government relief materials to countries in need. Developments since the end of the Cold War have clouded this process with more politically complex and dangerous operations in far greater frequency. These emergencies tend to occur more often in remote locations and in more chaotic conditions that require not only humanitarian assistance, but security for U.S. personnel and those receiving aid (Natsios 1997, 105-106). So, there are more operations, in more remote locations, under complex circumstances, involving more security issues. There are obviously greater costs associated with these new types of operations.

The U.S. military has not embraced its greater role with these operations, although many of the mass media images of U.S. humanitarian operations have shown a more compassionate view of the military. Resources diverted to these missions have come from limited military budgets and this ultimately detracts from combat readiness. It should be remembered that combat readiness, to ensure adequate protection of the country and U.S. interests, is the primary mission of the military (Natsios 1997, 111).

Risks

Potent risks are associated with U.S. policy to meet U.S. national security objectives regarding use of U.S. military forces in peacekeeping, peace-enforcement, and humanitarian operations. These risks can be potentially prohibitive if mass media highlights weak areas, actual or merely perceived, in a way that alters mission planning. Some of these risks deal with power structures, ethnic aspects of many crises, and political strategies being employed.

The power structures being used today to address problems related to international stability are much different than the power structures that were used to oversee the Cold War international system. The primary instability issue that confronts the international community today is political rather than technical (U.S. Congress 1995, 51). A weak international framework creates a situation whereby the potential pitfalls can be more numerous.

The ethnicization of politics evidences there is an ethnic aspect of the crisis situations in Europe and, equally important, a probability for the crises to be manipulated politically. As such, political leaders can exploit ethnic tensions in a crisis to better meet their own objectives (Alongi 1996, 193). Mass media channels offer avenues for such exploitation.

The link between humanitarian efforts by nongovernmental organizations and military participation with these missions can be fragile and problematic. Oftentimes the humanitarian intervention can become, intentionally or unintentionally, a political instrument associated with military objectives (Sahnoun 1998, 95). Mass media images of foreign civilians arriving to provide aid and comfort can easily be interpreted as a friendly international gesture. Mass media images of uniformed military troops, with weapons, can easily be interpreted as an occupying military force. The civilian and military objectives can be the same. The impressions created, and risks associated with the varied impressions, can be much different.

Military Readiness

A meaningful evaluation of military readiness is contingent upon a clear definition of mission objectives and the means to achieve the desired ends. This requires a strong link between the logic of political ends and the language of the military means toward those ends. Avoidance, or minimalization of, mission creep will be crucial in that military readiness can be diluted as the mission expands.

There are four crucial meeting points between the aforementioned political logic and military language. These points, in developmental order, are: (1) determining political ends; (2) aligning military means and political ends; (3)

political control (civilian political control of national militaries); and (4) consolidating a political outcome and disengagement (Whitman, 1997, 22-26).

The phenomenon of "mission creep" has received increased emphasis in the humanitarian lexicon over the past ten years as a result of expanding humanitarian operations that have occurred during that period. For instance, in the former Yugoslavia, "United Nations activity steadily escalated incrementally, from monitoring ceasefires . . . to launching a large, humanitarian mission . . . to deploying tens of thousands of peacekeepers to protect the UN humanitarian programs . . . to NATO forces replacing UN peacekeeping forces." (Rudolph 1997, 140). Missions can expand and almost take on a life of their own. The speed of mass media technologies can seemingly detract from critical thinking needed for rational decision making and, once the mission expands, it can be problematic to disengage from the commitment.

U.S. Public Support

U.S. public support is probably the most fickle criterion, regarding U.S. policy and U.S. national security strategy objectives, and most reliant on mass media channels to be successful (or unsuccessful). The public mind is fertile ground to be persuaded by general images rather than by specific factual data.

Persuasive images regarding the necessity for U.S. military intervention can be compelling. Such images can be based on the fairly new idea (in the history of humanity) that viewers are obligated to help other human beings simply because they are human (Ignatieff 1998, 287).

The humanitarian theme in such a narrative can be conveyed through literal spoken and written messages and visual images. "We are in one world; we must shoulder each other's fate; the value of life is indivisible. What happens to the starving in Africa and the homeless in Asia must concern all because we are all one species" (Ignatieff 1998, 290). Each mass media channel has unique strengths to promote this message. For instance, the overwhelming emotional impact of a televised visual image can override critical thinking by the U.S. public. Thus, U.S. leaders should consider U.S. public opinion in such matters but not necessarily consider it to be an informed or educated opinion.

Conclusions

This chapter has analyzed the impact of international peacekeeping, peace-enforcement, and humanitarian operations on U.S. national security strategy since 1992. This analysis focused on the consistent relevance of mass media and the role it plays regarding such variables as political considerations, human rights and military capabilities. A specific point illustrated in this study is that mass media affects the decision-making process related to the evolution of international peacekeeping, peace-enforcement, and humanitarian operations as tools linked to U.S. national security strategy.

The issues analysis section of this chapter dealt with political considerations, human rights, and military capabilities regarding their impact on the decision to employ U.S. forces in international peacekeeping, peacemaking, and humanitarian operations. Analysis confirmed the role mass media plays with the aforementioned variables. Examples supporting this position were drawn from U.S. military involvement in the former Yugoslavia, Somalia, and Rwanda.

U.S. policy, regarding the use of U.S. military forces in peacekeeping, peace-enforcement, and humanitarian operations to meet U.S. national security strategy objectives, was measured against the five criteria of national interests, costs, risks, military readiness, and U.S. public support in the policy evaluation section. This evaluation revealed and reinforced the importance of mass media interpretations of these criteria.

Recommendations

Recommendations based on the findings of this chapter stress the central theme of the need for critical thinking by U.S. decision makers when considering commitment of U.S. troops in international peacekeeping, peace-enforcement, and humanitarian operations. Such critical thinking is challenged, and at times undermined, by mass media influences. These influences typically stress appeals based on emotion rather than clearly developed logic.

The May 1997 publication of "A National Security Strategy for a New Century," prepared by the White House, gives a broad overview of national security variables but no concrete standard by which decisions can be made regarding the use of U.S. military in peacekeeping, peace-enforcement, and humanitarian operations. Similarly, the 1997 "National Military Strategy of the United States of America," submitted by General John Shalikashvili, conveys basic concerns and general guidance but does not provide clear criteria for the use of U.S. military in the aforementioned situations.

Thus, decision makers need concrete criteria for making such decisions, exceptions to said criteria should be stipulated, a process of checks and balances should be used to ensure criteria have been followed, and a thorough "lessons learned" assessment should be done when missions are completed to learn what worked and what did not. The assessment process would obviously benefit future planning when similar kinds of circumstances occur. Again, this process is recommended as a means to promote critical thinking in the decision-making process.

Regarding specifics of who, what, and how, a U.S. Military Humanitarian Mission Consideration Task Force could be convened to oversee each operation presented for consideration. Such a task force would have a representative from the military, State Department, White House administration, and NGO (nongovernmental organization) community. The function of the task force would be to gauge the necessity for U.S. military intervention by comparing the facts of the situation against criteria warranting U.S. involvement. Each task force member would represent the views of his or her constituency.

Their report would be submitted to the White House and the chairman of the Joint Chiefs of Staff, where ultimate decisions would be made. Said report would list criteria used for judging the situation, the primary factual data used by the task force, and a narrative explaining their findings. The president would not be bound by the task force recommendations but he or she could at least use them as a standard by which his/her decision could be contrasted.

This recommendation is meant to stress the need for critical thinking by decision makers to avoid pitfalls of making decisions based on emotion rather than logic. Mass media channels have a history of swaying public opinion, which, in turn, affects the actions of politicians who lead the nation. This swaying occurs because mass media images can be powerful on the emotional level but weak with factual data to support the main idea being purported. The aforementioned task force would seek to ensure critical thinking and consider input from various organizational perspectives that would be involved in the implementation of such a mission.

References

Alongi, M. 1996. *Conference Report—Ethnic Conflict and European Security: Lessons from the Past and Implications for the Future.* Strategic Studies Institute, U.S. Army War College, PA, October.

Annan, K. 1998. "Peacekeeping, military intervention, and national sovereignty in internal armed conflict." In *Hard Choices: Moral Dilemmas in Humanitarian Intervention*, ed. J. Moore. New York, Rowman & Littlefield.

Chopra, J., and T. J. Watson. 1997. "Background paper: political peace-maintenance in Somalia. In *Humanitarian Action and Peace-keeping Operations: Debriefing andLessons*, ed. N. Azimio, Boston: Kluwer Law International.

Clarke, W., and J. Herbst. 1997. "Somalia and the future of humanitarian intervention." *Learning from Somalia: The Lessons of Armed Humanitarian Intervention*, ed. W. Clarke, and J. Herbst, Boulder, CO: Westview Press.

Dallaire, R. A. 1998. "The end of innocence: Rwanda 1994." In *Hard Choices: Moral Dilemmas in Humanitarian Intervention*, ed. J. Moore. New York: Rowman & Littlefield.

Dole, B. "Atrocities in Kosovo," statement at a hearing before the Commission on Security and Cooperation in Europe, U.S. Congress, House, 105th Congress, 2d Session, September 17, 1998, Washington, GPO, 1999.

Dunn, D. H. 1996. "Anti-internationalism and the new American foreign policy debate." *Contemporary Security Policy*, 17 (2), (August): 238-63.

Giradet, E. R. 1996. "Reporting humanitarianism: Are the new electric media making a difference?" *From Massacres to Genocide*, ed. R. I. Rotberg, and T. G. Weiss. Cambridge MA: The World Peace Foundation.

Golden, J., et. al. 1997. *The Rhetoric of Western Thought*. Dubuque, IA: Kendall/Hunt.

Hackett, K. 1997. "Rwanda and Burundi: A future path for reconciliation in central Africa." In *The Politics of International Humanitarian Aid Operations*, ed. E.A. Belgrad and N. Nachmias. Westport, CT: Praeger.

Ignatieff, M. 1998. "The stories we tell: Television and humanitarian aid." In *Hard Choices: Moral Dilemmas in Humanitarian Intervention*, ed. J. Moore. New York: Rowman & Littlefield.

Ignatieff, M. 1997. *The Warrior's Honor*. New York: Metropolitan Books. Kagan, R. 1998. "The benevolent empire." *Foreign Policy*, (Summer): 24-34.

Leurdijk, R. A. 1997. "Background paper: United Nations protection force." In *Humanitarian Action and Peace-keeping Operations: Debriefing and Lessons*, ed. N. Azimo. Boston: Kluwer Law International.

McLean, D. 1996. *Peace Operations and Common Sense: Replacing Rhetoric with Realism*. Washington, DC: United States Institute of Peace.

Minear, L., and P. Guillot. 1996. *Soldiers to the Rescue: Humanitarian Lessons from Rwanda*. Paris: Organization for Economic Cooperation and Development.

Natsios, A.S. 1997. *U.S. Foreign Policy and the Four Horsemen of the Apocalypse*. Westport, CT: Praeger.

Posen, B. R. and A. L. Ross. "Competing visions for U.S. grand strategy." *International Security*, 21 (3), (Winter 1996/97): 5-53.

Rotberg, R. I. 1997. "The lessons of Somalia for the future of U.S. foreign policy." In *Learning From Somalia: The Lessons of Armed Humanitarian Intervention*, ed. W. Clarke and J. Herbst. Boulder, CO: Westview Press.

Rudolph, J. R. 1997. "Humanitarian aid in the former Yugoslavia: The limits of militarized humanitarian assistance." In *The Politics of International Humanitarian Aid Operations*, ed. E.A. Belgrad and N. Nachmias. Westport, CT:, Praeger.

Sahnoun, M. 1998. "Mixed Intervention in Somalia and the Great Lakes: Culture, neutrality and the military." In *Hard Choices: Moral Dilemmas in Humanitarian Intervention*, ed. J. Moore. New York: Rowman & Littlefield.

Smith, S., and J. Baylis. 1997. *The Globalization of World Politics: An Introduction to International Politics*. Oxford: Oxford University Press.

Snow, D. M., and Brown, E. 1997. *Beyond the Water's Edge: Introduction to U.S. Foreign Policy*. New York: St. Martin's Press.

Tedstrom, J. E. 1997. "NATO's economic challenges: Development and reform in East-Central Europe." *The Washington Quarterly*, 20 (2), (Spring): 3-19.

United States Congress, Office of Technology Assessment, *Improving the Prospects for Future International Peace Operations—Workshop Proceedings*, Washington GPO, 1995.

Whitman, J. 1997. "Military risk and political commitment in UN humanitarian peace support operations." In *The Politics of International Humanitarian Aid Operations*, ed. E. A. Belgrad and N. Nachmias. Westport, CT: Praeger.

Chapter Five

Understanding the Shock in "Culture Shock"

As international commerce and travel continues to flourish, we frequently find ourselves interacting with individuals who are culturally different from us. There are enrichments and frustrations that evolve from such encounters. "Culture shock" is the expression generally associated with the frustrations that occur when we have difficulty functioning in a different culture or when we are exposed to individuals from another culture. Note the latter situation does not necessitate our being in a foreign land. Culture shock can occur in our own hometowns and workplaces.

As a professor of interpersonal communication, most of my research deals with cross-cultural communication and how the communication process can be improved overall. The field has grown considerably since I completed my Ph.D. in 1982, but the focus on culture shock has been strong and steady since the beginnings of cross-cultural study. Culture shock is a phenomenon with very real and direct consequences but it can be interpreted and understood from a theoretical perspective.

As discussed in chapter one, culture shock typically occurs in a four-stage process that can unfold over varying lengths of time: the honeymoon, crisis, resolution, and stabilization stages. The honeymoon stage exists during our initial intrigue with a place, person or perspective that is culturally different but interesting to us. It is during this stage that we somewhat rejoice in that which is different. The crisis stage occurs when we are confronted with an event or situation that confuses us to such a degree that it becomes a significant obstacle. This confusion can typically lead to frustration and anger. The resolution stage begins when we start to develop a means for dealing with the obstacle encountered in the crisis stage. During this period we develop a resolution mechanism, or approach, that can be used when encountering future obstacles. The stabilization stage is the final period of culture shock when we have resolved the earlier confusion and have achieved a balanced outlook. The culture shock stages are exemplified in a situation I experienced as a visiting professor in China.

Honeymoon stage: During the early days of my first visit to China I was elated to be there and was very impressed with the people I met and was especially impressed with the diligence portrayed by my students.

Crisis stage: A significant problem arose when I discovered some of my students had plagiarized some of the material they included in their written reports for my class. That is, they included material authored by someone else without crediting authorship of the material, thus implying they wrote it. I was disturbed by this because they were fine people and I assumed my reporting the incident would result in their removal from the university.

Resolution stage: I did report the incident and learned the situation was not perceived to be a problem in China. In the United States we stress individual ownership of many things, including ideas. In this case we would expect ideas of others to be footnoted. In China, ideas, in this particular scenario, are recognized as belonging to the masses (that is, they belong to society) and there is not a stringent need to reference a source.

Stabilization stage: I bridged the U.S. and Chinese approaches for using the work of another person by telling my students if they come to the United States they must directly footnote external sources or they will suffer grave consequences. It was not an issue for me after that.

As indicated earlier you don't have to leave the United States to experience culture shock. I am a professor at a school in central Ohio and have culture shock experiences, similar to the aforementioned incident, that occur on my campus. Roughly 10 percent of our student body is from outside of the United States.

In the military context culture shock can occur in training situations that involve participants from different cultural backgrounds. I experienced culture shock in such a training situation that included Iranians during the summer of 1978 at a U.S. military installation (roughly a year before the 1979 Iranian revolution that resulted in U.S. and Iranian tensions).

Honeymoon stage: I lived next door to two Iranians, Ahmad and Yahdi, in base housing. We were attending the same school and I enjoyed learning about their culture during idle hours in the evening and on weekends.

Crisis stage: One evening, after I returned from the library, I smelled an unusual odor coming from the bathroom that Ahmad and I shared. The bathroom was located between our bedrooms and we each had an entrance. There was also loud obnoxious music coming from his room. I entered the bathroom and found the sink and bathtub contained what I can best describe as smelly food scraps. They smelled very bad. I opened his door and found he and Yahdi were preparing a large meal and had some unappealing (to my ears) music blaring. I had planned to shave, shower, and study the rest of the evening but this situation stopped me in my tracks. They were oblivious to my concerns about the smell and sound. I considered moving to another room but was aware our building was full. I shaved at a sink in the janitor's closet, was not able to shower, was not able to study because of the music, and had trouble sleeping because of the smell. I was tired and irritable the next day and didn't speak to them.

Resolution stage: I noticed the next evening that the bathroom was clean and there was no loud music playing in Ahmad's room. Late in the evening I saw Ahmad in the hallway and he acted as if the previous evening's confusion had not occurred. As I visited with him I realized the confusion had not occurred for him. He was unaware of my anger until I explained my perception of the situation. He explained it was some type of holy day for them and that it was common for them to engage in that behavior during such days. I was comforted to know it would not happen often.

Stabilization stage: I asked Ahmad to give me advance notice before similar unusual events occurred in the future. This would allow me to plan accordingly and avoid disruption. He honored my request. It turned out to be a learning experience as I learned a little about their holy days and how they observed them.

The key to successfully dealing with culture shock rests with being able to recognize the stages of culture shock as you experience them. This will allow you to be more rationale in your responses to what you encounter. If you experience frustration but can rationally understand why you are frustrated, this can help reduce the anxiety.

During a visit to Senegal (West Africa) I became fearful when I perceived many people were staring at me. I interpreted their stares as being a threat until I thought about the situation and realized I was the only white person in the area, and I was dressed different than they were. It was understandable for them to be curious about me.

Recognizing culture shock won't make it totally disappear but, like many problems, recognition is the first step toward understanding. Once you understand the shock in "culture shock" you can change it from a frustrating experience to a learning experience.

Chapter Six

Applied Interpersonal Communication in a Cross-Cultural Context: The Use of Interpreters as an Interrogation Technique When Interviewing Spanish-Speaking Individuals

The intelligence community of the U.S. military collects information in a variety of ways. This chapter will focus on the collection of information from human sources, specifically, sources who require the use of a Spanish-speaking interpreter. However, the dynamics to be covered would be relevant with a source speaking any foreign language.

While the term interrogation sometimes conjures visions of physical coercion, this chapter will deal with the process as applied interpersonal communication in a cross-cultural context, as approved by the Geneva Conventions. The primary source of information used in this chapter is Field Manual 34-52, *Intelligence Interrogation,* published by the Department of the Army in May 1987. Information presented is unclassified and is approved for public release. Distribution is unlimited. My analysis of this topic should not be construed as an endorsement for such activity. I am interested in said study as a form of case study analysis.

I have completed the basic interrogation course offered by the Department of the Army and received additional interrogation training in Human Relations Intelligence (HUMINT) from the Air Force. It will be helpful to describe primary considerations in the interrogation process before addressing the specific use of an interpreter. This discussion will provide a relevant backdrop for interpreter use issues.

Interrogation is "the art of questioning and examining a source to obtain the maximum amount of usable information." Sources may be civilian internees, insurgents, defectors, refugees, displaced persons, and agents or suspected agents. The goal of any interrogation is "to obtain usable and reliable information, in a lawful manner and in the least amount of time, which meets intelligence requirements of any echelon of command." The interrogation should produce information that is "timely, complete, clear, and accurate" (Field Manual 1987, 81).

There are four principles of interrogation: initiative, accuracy, prohibition against force, and security (Field Manual 1987). These principles apply to any type of intelligence/interrogation. Each interrogation has a definite objective, based on the collection of information that will satisfy the intelligence needs of the supported unit's mission. The interrogation must regard this objective as primary. It will serve as a basis for planning and conducting the interrogation.

Initiative is emphasized as the interrogator must remain in charge throughout the interrogation. If the source is able to take control of the interrogation, this can have a direct negative impact on the information gathering process.

The interrogator must show concern for obtaining accurate information from the source. A common procedure is to repeat questions at varying intervals. However, the interrogator should not try to act as an analyst. His or her primary mission is to collect information, but not evaluate it.

The use of force is prohibited at all times in the interrogation process. It is prohibited by law and is neither authorized nor condoned by the U.S. government. The use of force is also inefficient as it can force the source to say whatever he or she thinks the interrogator wants to hear.

The interrogator must be aware of security issues relevant to his or her position. He or she works with a great deal of classified information and must be careful not to reveal such information to sources. He or she must also be sensitive to any attempts by sources to elicit information.

The aforementioned principles of interrogation provide general areas that the interrogator must be concerned with as he or she works to conduct a successful interrogation. Additionally, there are five primary interrogation phases that emphasize more specific details regarding the collection of information: planning and preparation, approach, questioning, termination, and reporting (Field Manual 1987).

The planning and preparation phase lays the groundwork for the interrogation process. Considerations in this procedure include the source's mental and physical condition, the source's background, the objective of the interrogation, and the interrelationship of source and interrogator personalities. The questioning of guards, for example, helps the interrogator learn about the source before meeting him or her face-to-face.

The approach phase is unique to each interrogation but all approaches share a number of common purposes: establish and maintain control, establish and maintain rapport, and manipulation of the source's emotions and weaknesses to gain his or her willing cooperation. This phase is based on appropriate source assessment, smooth transitions, and recognition of source breaking point.

The questioning phase usually begins when the source starts to answer questions relevant to specific interrogation objectives, although he or she may have already answered less pertinent questions. There are many areas of emphasis in this phase, such as the use of direct questions, appropriate follow-up questions, repeating questions to insure accuracy, and avoidance of ambiguous or leading questions. Map tracking (using a map to pinpoint specific locations and progressions) is helpful in insuring consistency, accuracy, and understanding in this phase.

The termination phase can be initiated for a variety of reasons: the source is uncooperative, all pertinent information has been obtained, time constraints, and so on. This phase should be conducted without any loss of rapport since the source may be questioned again by the same interrogator or a different interrogator. He or she should be told his or her information will be checked for truthfulness and a final opportunity to change or add any information should be offered.

The final phase involves reporting information of intelligence value to the appropriate agency. Each military branch dictates the types of forms and procedures used in this phase. Regardless, reporting information should not be confused with evaluating information.

If the interrogator does not speak the source's language, then an interpreter must use used. Thus, the interrogation process becomes applied interpersonal communication in a cross-cultural context involving a third party, the third party being fluent in the languages spoke by the interrogator and the source.

Interrogation of Spanish-speaking sources by English-speaking interrogators, using bilingual (English-Spanish) interpreters, continues to be a realistic scenario due to continued U.S. involvement in Central America. Analysis of this interrogation situation evidences the need for interpersonal sensitivity by the interrogator.

Using an interpreter is a lengthy process since the interpreter must repeat everything said by the interrogator and the source. This requires considerable understanding between the interrogator and the interpreter.

Verbal and nonverbal communication elements are central to a successful interrogation using an interpreter. A primary verbal concern deals with the approach used by the interpreter to convey interrogator statements. Nonverbal concerns deal with vocalics, proxemics, occulesics, and kinesic considerations. The interpreter needs to serve as a bridge of understanding, verbally and nonverbally, between interrogator and source.

A fundamental tenet of this process dictates the source must understand that the interrogator, not the interpreter, is in charge. This receives equal emphasis in the verbal and nonverbal areas. There are two methods of interpretation: simultaneous and alternate. Using the simultaneous method, the interpreter listens and translates at the same time the interrogator speaks. Using the alternate method, the interpreter listens to an entire phrase (paragraph, and so forth) and periodically translates during natural pauses. The simultaneous method should be used only if the sentence structure of the source language is parallel to English, the interpreter can easily imitate the interrogator's tone and attitude, and the interpreter is very fluent in both languages.

Vocalic considerations emphasize that the interpreter needs to use interrogation content, tone of voice, inflection, and intent. He or she should not inject any of his or her own personality or ideas.

Proxemic concerns focus on the physical arrangement of the three individuals. The preferred arrangement is to have the interrogator and source facing each other with the interpreter behind the source. This improves the interrogator's control as he or she can simultaneously interact with the source and interpreter. This also discourages the source from fixating on the interpreter as a person.

When the interrogator first meets with the source, the source should be instructed to maintain eye contact with the interrogator. Eye contact (occulesics) helps build a strong base of rapport between interrogator and source.

Kinesics deals with various types of body movements (Schnell 1996). Kinesics is especially important in situations when the source must look at the interpreter, such as map tracking for instance. During such times, the interpreter should imitate the kinesic behaviors of the interrogator as closely as possible. Otherwise, contradictory messages can be sent.

Prior to the interrogation, the interrogator should learn as much as possible about the nonverbal behavior norms of the source's home country. Knowledge of nonverbal behaviors can become very important since nonverbal norms are uniquely grounded in each culture. Thus, the interrogator who is insensitive to source nonverbal norms may unknowingly send contradictory meanings. Physical distance, body gestures, eye contact, pauses, and clothing, for instance, affect the nonverbal climate in which the interrogation takes place (Schnell 1996). Thus, the informed interrogator should be aware of proxemic, kinesic, occulesic, vocalic, and objectic norms of the source's native country.

More than twenty approaches can be used when constructing the question sequence and desired interpersonal climate of the interrogation. Each approach dictates definite behaviors that must be communicated, verbally and nonverbally, by the interrogator (and through his or her interpreter).

The most common, and most successful, approach is called the "direct approach." Ironically, the direct approach is frequently referred to as no approach at all. Just as the name implies, it merely involves asking questions in a straightforward manner. Due to its effectiveness, and simplicity, the direct approach should be used first.

Beyond the direct approach, the approaches vary considerably in intensity and complexity, as exemplified in the following descriptions. These approaches can be stressed individually or blended with other approaches. A decision to blend approaches will depend on the unique circumstances of the situation.

The *incentive approach* involves rewarding the source for his or her cooperation. It is important to ensure the rewards serve to reinforce positive behavior.

The *emotional hate approach* focuses on the source's bitter feelings toward his or her superiors, fellow soldiers, unit or country. For example, this approach might be effective with a source who has been conscripted and forced into battle.

The *pride and ego down approach* is based on the interrogator attacking the source's sense of personal worth. For instance, questioning his or her ability as a soldier for letting him or herself be captured and how he or she might have negatively affected his or her unit and fellow soldiers.

The *file and dossier approach* is when the interrogator convinces the source that he or she already knows everything about the source and just needs to find out some minor details. This approach is based on strategic exaggeration and manipulation of what little information the interrogator might have about the source.

Again, there are a wide variety of approaches and the aforementioned exemplify some of the more common ones. Each approach dictates different emphasis on interpersonal communication variables.

The interrogation process is a very complicated form of interpersonal communication. The process is further complicated when the interrogator and source are from different countries and do not share common communication norms. The process becomes even more complicated when the interrogator and source do not speak the same language and a third party is introduced to interpret.

The use of bilingual interpreters, when used correctly, definitely enhances applied interpersonal communication in this cross-cultural context. The examples discussed in this chapter are especially unique due to the complexity of the interpersonal exchange described.

References

Field Manual 34-52. 1987. *Intelligence Interrogation: An Applied Field Manual To Aid in the Collection, Organization, Analysis and Reporting of Information Gained from Human Subjects.* Department of the Army (May).

Schnell, J. A. 1996. *Interpersonal Communication: Understanding and Being Understood*. East Rockaway, NY: Cummings and Hathaway Publishers.

Chapter Seven

Neoauthoritarian Journalistic Approaches Used by the Chinese Government during the 1996 Taiwan Controversy

During the period of George Washington's leadership (1770s) China was governed by the Qianlong emperor. Washington exhibited minimal influence over what journalists wrote but this was not the practice of his contemporary halfway around the world. The Qianlong emperor maintained strict control over what Chinese writers produced. "A dictionary maker named Wang Xihou was found to have included in his dictionary the taboo temple names of the Qing emperors, so he was executed and twenty-one members of his family were enslaved. The provincial governor who had supported the publication was also executed" (Fairbank 1990, ix).

This scenario exemplifies how different the United States and China were in the area of journalistic freedom. Significant differences and parallels to that time period still exist today. "Just because most of us don't spend our time thinking about the past doesn't mean the past does not constantly influence the present. China's modern media have grown up and operate today in the shadow of China's long heritage of central autocracy" (Fairbank 1990, x). Today the central government autocracy expresses itself through a form of neoauthoritarian leadership. This phenomenon is relevant to us today because with increased U.S.-China trade and interaction we will be affected by these practices.

Neoauthoritarianism has been used as a unique strategy by the Chinese leadership to govern the modernization of Chinese society. Neoauthoritarianism posits political dictatorship and economic freedom can coexist within a society (Huntington 1968). This inquiry focuses on Chinese neoauthoritarian journalistic approaches practiced during the 1996 Taiwan sovereignty/reunification controversy.

In March 1996, *U.S. News & World Report* reported:

A map of Taiwan suddenly filled the screen during the Chinese television news one evening last week. As a somber announcer began to read latitudinal and

longitudinal coordinates of missile tests near Taiwan a red box appeared on the
map at the northeast tip of the island to mark one target zone. A second red box
appeared southwest of the island. As the announcer read on, the boxes began
flashing angrily. (Lawrence and Palmer 1996, 53)

I, and millions of Chinese citizens, saw this report as I ate dinner in Beijing, the
capital of China.

I was in China during the period of the Chinese military exercises held in the
Taiwan Straits and used this opportunity to gather data dealing with
communicative efforts by the Chinese government to influence perceptions of
in-country U.S. citizens, regarding U.S. credibility and intentions, related to the
Taiwan sovereignty/reunification controversy. The exercises were staged to
dampen the first-ever Taiwanese presidential elections on March 23, 1996. It
was my sixth visit to China, where I have been a visiting professor at a
university in Beijing.

The Chinese government uses three government-owned and government
controlled media channels to convey messages to English-speaking foreigners
(including U.S. citizens) who are in China. These channels are newspaper,
television, and radio. China Central Television (CCTV) broadcasts English
language news Monday through Friday at 9 P.M., 4 P.M. and 11 P.M. on channel
9. Each news report is about fifteen minutes in length. China Radio International
(CRI) broadcasts English news periodically throughout the day on 91.5 FM.
Each news report lasts about ten minutes.

China Daily is an English language newspaper that is published Monday
through Saturday. It typically consists of about eight pages and is "China's
national English language newspaper" *("China Daily,*1996). It began
publication in June 1981. The main office is in Beijing and there are seven
regional offices throughout China.

Between February 21 and March 18, 1996, I listened to CRI radio news each
day, watched CCTV news each day it was broadcast, and read *China Daily* six
days a week. I analyzed the broadcasts and newspaper reports for information
that conveyed representative references to U.S. credibility and intentions
regarding the Taiwan sovereignty/reunification controversy related to People's
Liberation Army exercises in the Taiwan Straits. The most relevant period of
reporting during this time frame was between March 6, when the military
exercises were announced, and March 18.

Significant news information released by *China Daily*, CRI, and CCTV is
controlled by the Xinhua News Agency. It is the central approving authority for
news. Thus, significant news information conveyed on CCTV and CRI is also
reported in *China Daily*. Reporting in *China Daily* is more extensive than CCTV
and CRI, because of its newspaper format, so I focused on collecting
representative references from *China Daily*. A month before arriving in China I

was a visiting fellow at the East-West Center in Honolulu and met a *China Daily* journalist there. He confirmed the role of the Xinhua News Agency.

This phenomena can be interpreted using a journalistic paradigm stressing neoauthoritarianism. This perspective is especially relevant for interpreting developments in China.

Chan and Lee define a journalistic paradigm as readily accepted "assumptions or gestalt world views that inform the media as to what social facts to report (and what not to report) and how to interpret them" (1984, 139). The journalistic paradigm offers a frame of reference that all information can be placed within and ascribed as part of the social order. Such a perspective allows the media to construct realities that the consumer can use to interpret events (Chan and Lee, 1988).

The perpetuation of a unified frame of reference in China is described by Ruan Ming. Ming states "the Party's own establishment, the new People's Republic, betrays Marx and denies press freedom in order to maintain 'unified public opinion.' This republic is thus a fake; it is Mao's empire of 'one leader, one ideology, and one party'" (1990, 123). He uses this position as a foundation for his explanation of neoauthoritarianism in China.

The central premise of neoauthoritarianism is that political dictatorship and economic freedom can exist within the same social order (Huntington 1968). The main idea behind the theory, as explained by former Premier Zhao Ziyang, is that "in underdeveloped countries, the process of modernization should be carried out through iron-fisted political dictatorship rather than through western-style democracy" (*China Tribune* 1989, 3). The theoretical framework for such a system would encourage increased wealth for successful individuals, but only within the political control of the communist leadership.

Such an orientation offers partial linkage with previously discouraged western ideology. As such, "western ideology is not a set of clearly articulated principles and standards. Rather, it is presented as a lifestyle of unmistakable affluence. . . . is a sharp contrast between what they see around them in their own lives and what they see on the video screens" (Chu and Yanan 1993, 13).

Neoauthoritarianism promotes economic initiatives by the individual but allows minimal political freedoms to be enjoyed by the individual. Journalistic freedoms, for example, are significantly curbed to adherence with the Chinese leadership views to the point that journalistic outlets can be defined as propaganda organs. Thus, analysis of *China Daily*, CRI and CCTV must be done with the aforementioned neoauthoritarian construct realized.

Thirty-two articles were collected during the twenty-seven day (February 21-March 18, 1996) time frame. This chapter will describe representative articles, in chronological order, that address U.S. credibility and intentions, with regard to the Taiwan issue. Since these stories were conveyed via English language channels, it can be assumed the in-country U.S. citizens were targeted with this information.

On March 4, 1996, two days before the military exercises were announced, *China Daily* published an opinion article by Yan Xuetong, deputy director of the Centre for China's Foreign Policy Studies, titled "China's Security Goals Do Not Pose a Threat to World, Analyst Says." In the article, Yan explains, "If the U.S. stops its (arms) sales (to Taiwan), the peaceful reunification process (between China and Taiwan) will be accelerated. . . . China's nationalism has always been characterized by self-salvation instead of the egoistic tendency of western countries. . . . only by preventing the arms sales by the U.S. to Taiwan can the peaceful reunification of the country be realized" (Yan 1996).

Also on March 4 a short article excerpted a story that had been published in *People's Daily* (the largest Chinese language newspaper published in China). The story briefly describes how U.S. diplomacy failed to create support for its position against Cuba when the United States was criticizing Cuba for downing two U.S.-registered planes, owned by Cuban dissidents living in the United States, that had invaded Cuban air space. "However, the United States failed to get wide international support it had expected" (*China Daily* 1996). This article is relevant because it provided context for the criticisms, lodged against the United States by China two days later, regarding U.S. diplomatic interference with Taiwan's move toward sovereignty, the implication being U.S. diplomacy is consistently at fault.

On March 6 a front-page article, featuring a map of Taiwan, announced missile tests to be conducted March 8-15 in the sea area near Taiwan. The article stated, "As long as . . . foreign powers, including the United States, stop arms sales to Taiwan, the tension will be relaxed" (*China Daily* 1996). The same day, a lengthy article, excerpting a report delivered by Premier Li Peng to the Fourth Session of the Eighth National People's Congress, stated: "Only when the principles enunciated in the three Sino-U.S. joint communiques are strictly observed and only when the two sides respect each other and refrain from interfering in each other's internal affairs will Sino-U.S. relations achieve sound development" (*China Daily* 1996).

The military exercises near Taiwan began on March 8, and three articles that criticized U.S. foreign policy (an unusually high number of such articles) appeared on the same day. One article protested a U.S. State Department report that was critical of human rights abuses in China. It stated the United States should "do away with its wrongful practices of making unwarranted charges against other countries' human rights situations" and went on to label the missile tests as "a normal exercise designed to improve the military quality of the

Chinese servicemen (Xu 1996). Another article was also critical of the United States because facts had surfaced "that show a U.S. report on China's treatment of handicapped children to be a distortion" (*China Daily* 1996).

A third article on that day, entitled "U.S. Still Uses Power Politics," describes how the United States has been at fault in its relations with Cuba. "The U.S. wants to cook up the incident to convert the attitudes of the international community. . . . The fruitless sanctions of the U.S. against Cuba also show the weaknesses and incompatibleness of the only superpower in the changing world" (Chen, 1996). Parallels can be recognized between U.S. interference with Cuba and U.S. interference with the China-Taiwan issue.

The March 11 *China Daily* carried a short article and map that described how the Chinese military would be holding additional naval and air exercises in the Taiwan Straits between March 12-20 (China Daily 1996). A lengthy article (roughly 5,500 words) was included in the same issue, titled "Human Rights in China and U.S. Compared." The purpose of this article seems to be to criticize the United States for intervening in the internal affairs of another country, and it adds weight to its position by questioning the internal practices of the United States. However, the legitimacy of some of the statements made would probably be suspect in the eyes of most U.S. citizens.

The article begins by saying "American politicians have used the U.S. as a 'world human rights model' while wantonly attacking China's record on human rights" (*China Daily* 1996). "Compared with the U.S., the constitutional rights of Chinese citizens are much more extensive and specific. . . . The Congress of the U.S. belongs to, is ruled by, and serves the interests of the rich. . . . Slavery did not die out completely. The Mississippi state legislature did not pass a law abolishing slavery until as late as February 1995. . . . The top one percent of the population owns 40 percent of the country's wealth. . . . Half of the American people are illiterate. . . . One third of all U.S. women will be attacked by their partners. Moreover, 15-25 percent of pregnant women are beaten. . . ." (*China Daily* 1996).

The next day, March 12, three articles directly and indirectly address U.S. intervention in the Taiwan Straits. The boldest article assesses, "It was ridiculous that some people in the U.S. declared that the aircraft carrier Independence of the Seventh Fleet should sail towards Taiwan from its base in Japan, for intervention and even for defending Taiwan. . . . I think these people must have forgotten that Taiwan is a part of China's territory. It is not a protectorate of the U.S. . . . If they support Taiwan separatists' efforts, there will be a 'chaotic situation' . . . . an erroneous decision by the U.S. government in allowing Taiwan's Lee Teng-hui to visit the U.S. has since changed the once calm cross-Straits relations" (Ma 1996).

A related article adds, "It seems quite a few people from the west have a misunderstanding of the Chinese Army and that the mass media in the west have distorted the news about China in their reports" (*China Daily* 1996). The third article concludes, "We mean what we say should foreign interference or 'Taiwan independence' appear some day: We will use all possible means to safeguard the unity of our country" (*China Daily* 1996).

Two articles appeared on March 13 that provide fairly concrete analysis of the situation. "The U.S. was warned yesterday by the Foreign Ministry to stop backing Taiwan's separatist activities. . . . It will be very dangerous if the Taiwan leaders interpret this signal as the U.S. Government's support and encouragement for its activities to split China. . . . (referring to the U.S. Civil War). The U.S. also opposed outside interference, stressed national sovereignty and territorial integrity and was strongly against the sale of arms by a certain European country to the south" (Xu 1996).

A second article, also on the front page, establishes China's position. "There are two necessary conditions for peaceful settlement of the Taiwan question. . . . First, that Taiwan refrain from independence and separation; and second, that foreign governments not interfere in China's internal affairs and allow the Chinese people to settle the question on their own" (*China Daily* 1996). These two conditions have consistently been stressed over the past 25 years.

The following day, further elaboration on the Chinese government position was provided. "Relations across the Taiwan Straits have always been haunted by the shadow of the U.S. . . . the U.S. may base its support for Taiwan on various excuses such as 'traditional obligations,' but the bottom line is that it is unwilling to see a powerful and unified China and wants to use Taiwan to contain China . . . . U.S. and Taiwanese politicians should not misinterpret the justification and determination of the Chinese across the Taiwan Straits over reunification" (Guang 1996).

On March 14, more speculation and opinion on U.S. motivations are described. "The world should be alerted to the fact a few powers are using human rights issues as a weapon against developing countries. . . . But some western governments are not happy to see a China that enjoys political stability and sticks to the socialist course. The U.S. and other western countries. . . . turn a blind eye to their own problems while attacking China for its 'poor human rights record.' By doing so, they are trying to change China's political and social system which is the Chinese people's own choice" (Chen 1996). This reiterates the importance of Chinese autonomy.

Perhaps one of the most confusing articles, for the U.S. reader, appeared on March 15. The article opens and continues with "China urges the U.S. Government to 'take prompt and effective measures' to prevent the adoption of an anti-China bill in the House of Representatives. . . . We hereby express our firm opposition and strong indignation at it. . . . He blamed the U.S. naval fleet for causing setbacks to the stock market in Taiwan. When the U.S. conducts military exercises, no other country sends aircraft carriers to the region" (Xu 1996). The article is confusing because it never describes what the anti-China bill is. The reader can only speculate it might have something to do with the U.S. sending Navy ships to the Taiwan Straits.

Two front-page articles on March 16 briefly describe completion of missile tests in the Taiwan Straits and new exercises to be conducted in the area between March 18-25. The articles made no mention of foreign interference. However, another front-page article "accused the U.S. of adopting a double standard on wheat quarantine 'for its own interests.' It criticized the U.S. for what it described as a hegemonic act" (*China Daily* 1996).

A March 18 article resumed emphasis on China's position. "Any show of force by foreign powers in the Taiwan Straits will only deteriorate the situation. . . . Li (Premier Li Peng) declared that China would never accept the practice of others 'imposing one's will upon another'" (*China Daily* 1996).

On the same day a new topic was introduced regarding Chinese use of arms with the Taiwan situation. "A spokesman for the Chinese foreign ministry on Saturday refuted a report alleging that China has told the U.S. it will not resort to the use of arms in the Taiwan issue. . . . China has never promised to abstain from resorting to arms. . . . If something like 'Taiwan independence' or violation of Taiwanese space by a foreign force should occur, we certainly will use every means necessary to safeguard the sovereignty and territorial integrity of the motherland" (*China Daily* 1996).

Throughout the period data was collected for this study, I watched for direct (low context) criticisms of U.S. actions in support of Taiwan and more indirect (high context) meanings that reflect unfavorably on U.S. foreign policy and the United States overall. This inquiry revealed both kinds of messages were conveyed.

Low context messages, which are direct and explicitly stated, rely very little on the context provided in the situation, whereas high context messages, which are indirect and implicitly stated, draw much of their meaning from the context or situation within which they are conveyed. The high context meaning is portrayed more figuratively, much like a picture, and the low context message is spelled out with explicit wording in a literal sense. Consideration of low context and high context messaging is relevant, because China tends to be more high context oriented and the United. States tends to be more low context in the way meanings are conveyed (Hall 1984). Thus, the Chinese media must consider the importance of broadcasting information using a low context approach so that the American audience will correctly perceive messages as intended (as well as other English-speaking receivers of such information).

The influence of the messages described in this article, regarding U.S. credibility and intention related to the Taiwan controversy, would vary depending primarily on the sophistication of the American news consumer. That is, the U.S. citizen who recognizes Chinese English language media as government-controlled news organs can more realistically interpret messages as being interpretations preferred by the Chinese government rather than objective news reporting. The U.S. citizen who interprets Chinese English language media the same way he or she would interpret U.S. media (that is, not recognizing Chinese English language media are propaganda vehicles) will be more inclined to be misguided in learning the facts of a situation. Similarly, a more sophisticated American television viewer will see a network news documentary as being more objective than a thirty-minute paid political program sponsored by a political candidate.

Even when the U.S. citizen (in China) is aware of the aforementioned distinctions, he or she can be unduly influenced if he or she is exposed only to Chinese English language media and no (or little) information from non-Chinese sources. When I am in China I frequently listen to CRI news, watch CCTV news, and read *China Daily* because I do not have easy access to non-Chinese media and, even though I know it is government-controlled propaganda, I consume the media with the intention of "reading between the lines" (inferring from what is reported) to speculate on what the facts of the situation are.

This approach is not always effective, though. I was in China during the 1991 Persian Gulf War and the Chinese government perspective of the war, as conveyed through Chinese media, was different than what was reported in the western "free press." Not until after leaving China did I learn the degree to which the United States had international support for its actions. Even when media are recognized as propaganda, they still impact the perception of the receiver.

Thus, Chinese media portrayal of U.S. credibility and intentions regarding the Taiwan issue likely affected the perception of in-country U.S. citizens who consumed Chinese media and did not have easy access to western media. Again, the degree to which such Chinese media would be successful in conveying preferred meanings would primarily be based on the receiver's ability to consistently interpret the Chinese media as government propaganda, rather than as being produced by an independent free press. The aforementioned journalistic paradigm, acknowledging authoritarian practices, offers a framework for understanding communicative efforts by the Chinese government to influence perceptions of in-country U.S. citizens, regarding U.S. credibility and intentions, during the 1996 Taiwan sovereignty/reunification controversy. The media, via CRI, CCTV and *China Daily*, conveyed a unified interpretation of events related to the situation in the Taiwan Straits. During a period of longstanding economic growth, the central government was able to minimize political developments in China as exemplified by their ability to tightly control media reporting of the Taiwan controversy. Thus, given their success using a neoauthoritarian approach to promote economic growth (while minimizing political change), one can readily speculate this neoauthoritarian approach will continue to be practiced.

Still, China is caught in a balancing act between seeking foreign technology and trade it needs to stimulate economic growth and avoiding unwanted political ideas that filter into Chinese society in the process. This balancing act is apparent in that it could close its doors to the outside world, allowing the government to curb unwanted political influences, but doing so would result in China falling behind economically.

References

"Army Holds Naval and Air Exercises," *China Daily*, 11 March 1996, p. 1.

"Beijing Charges 'Double Standard' on U.S. Grain," *China Daily, XVI* March 1996, p. 1.

Chan, J.M. and Lee, C.C. 1984. "Journalistic Paradigms on Civil Protests: A Case Study in Hong Kong," in A. Arno and W. Dissanayake, eds. *The News Media in National and International Conflict*. Boulder, CO: Westview.

Chan, J.M. and Lee, C.C. 1987. "Journalistic Paradigms in Flux: Press and Political Transition in Hong Kong," *Bulletin of the Institute of Ethnology Academia Sinica* 63 (Spring): 109-131.

Chen, Y. "China Respects Human Rights," *China Daily,* 14 March 1996, p. 4.

Chen, Y. "U.S. Still Uses Power Politics," *China Daily,* 8 March 1996, p. 4.

"China Daily," *China Daily*, 6 March 1966, p. 4.

"China Makes a Move," *China Tribune,* 8 April 1989, p. 3.

Chu, G. and Yanan, J. 1993. *The Great Wall in Ruins: Communication and Cultural Change in China*. Albany: State University of New York Press.

Fairbank, J.K. 1990. "Foreword," in C.C. Lee, ed., *Voices of China: The Interplay of Politics and Journalism*. New York: Guilford Press.

Guang, L. "Separatists Responsible for Cross-Straits Tension," *China Daily*, 13 March 1996, p. 4.

Hall, E.T. 1984. *The Dance of Life: The Other Dimension of Time*. Garden City: Anchor Press.

"Human Rights in China and U.S. Compared," *China Daily,* 11 March 1996, p. 3.

Huntington, S. 1968. *Political Order in Changing Societies*. New Haven, CT: Yale University Press.

Lawrence, S.V. and Palmer, B. "China Practices Pulling the Trigger," *U.S. News & World Report,* 18 March 1996: 53-54.

"Li Explains Major Issues at NPC," *China Daily,* 6 March 1996, p. 4.

Ma, C. "China Resolved to Safeguard Sovereignty," *China Daily,* 12 March 1996, p. 1.

Ming, R. 1990. "Press Freedom and Neoauthoritarianism: A Reflection on China's Democracy Movement," in C.C. Lee, ed., *Voices of China: The Interplay of Politics and Journalism.* New York: Guilford Press.

"Missile Tests Improve Troop Skills," *China Daily,* 16 March 1996, p. 1.

"Missile Tests to Take Place in Areas Near Taiwan," *China Daily,* 6 March 1996, p. 1.

"New Military Exercises Announced," *China Daily,* 16 March 1996, p. 1.

"Official Refutes U.S. Report On Child Abuse," *China Daily*, 8 March 1996, p. 4.

"'One China' Key To Straits Negotiation," *China Daily*, 13 March 1996, p. 1.

"Policy on Taiwan Never To Change, Premier Says," *China Daily*, 18 March 1996, p. 2.

"Politics Behind Worsening U.S.-Cuba Ties," *China Daily*, 4 March 1996, p. 4.

"Separatism Blamed For Taiwan's Recent Woes," *China Daily*, 12 March 1996, p. 4.

"U.S. Assertion Groundless," *China Daily*, 18 March 1996, p. 1.

"Western 'China Threat' Myth Groundless," *China Daily,* 12 March 1996, p. 4.

Xu, Y. "China Protests U.S. Report on Human Rights," *China Daily,* 8 March 1996, p.1.

Xu, Y. "U.S. Told to End Its Support for Taiwanese Separatists," *China Daily,* 13 March 1996, p. 1.

Xu, Y. "U.S. Urged to Reject Anti-China Proposal," *China Daily,* 15 March 1996, p. 1.

Yan, X. "China's Security Goals Do Not Pose a Threat to World, Analyst Says," *China Daily,* 4 March 1996, p. 4.

Chapter 8

In Search of Afrocentric Perspectives on Human Communication

This chapter focuses on my efforts to locate, understand, and incorporate Afrocentric perspectives on human communication in my teaching of communication arts curriculum courses. It has been a lengthy, thorough, and thought-provoking experience. Multiculturalism is a controversial topic in education, and inclusion of Afrocentric scholarship is an element of that controversy. Objectivity is a high priority when doing research but, due to the nature of the content of this chapter, a brief description of my background is appropriate.

I am a white, male, middle-age professor at a small liberal arts college in Ohio. I completed my Ph.D. in 1982 and am an active researcher in cross-cultural communication. My interest with African-American scholarship grew from an awareness that pressures from multiculturalists may result in strong encouragement to modify the communication arts curriculum, a genuine curiosity in what Afrocentric perspectives are (and how they differ from what I currently teach), and a grant that supported my study of the aforementioned. I did not come into this project with a political agenda (I am politically moderate), and I do not have a hidden agenda in writing this chapter. It is merely a report of my findings.

My study of the subject began in the summer of 1991 when my college received a grant from the Lilly Foundation to, among other things, promote inclusion of African-American scholarship in the curriculum. My research included six visits to Howard University in Washington, D.C., recognized as the leading predominantly black college in the United States. My visits to Howard included sitting in on classes, meeting with faculty and students, and most importantly, studying African-American scholarship in the Moorland-Spingarn Research Center.

The Moorland-Spingarn Research Center is the "largest and the most valuable research library in America for the study of Negro life and history" and "the most comprehensive and interesting group of books by Negroes ever collected in the world" (*The Arthur B. Spingarn Collection of Negro Authors*

1947, 1, 7). Such a comprehensive collection of African-American scholarship offers a unique opportunity to study African-American contributions in a variety of areas. My study at the center is the foundation for the findings reported in this chapter. Since it is recognized as the largest collection of African-American scholarship in the United States, I view it as a collective voice for African-American thought.

It is speculated that by the year 2000 33 percent of school age children in the United States will be of non-European origin. Thus, there is a belief that our academic curriculums should be representative of these non-European perspectives. Thorough modifications will be a lengthy process. Calls for a more inclusive curriculum, representative of the multicultural composition of American society, have come from a variety of sources (Williams 1990; Viadero 1992; Gordon and Bhattacharyya 1992). One frequently hears that we need emphasis on education as a means to help American society get along with itself (in the area of interracial/ethnic relations). One can speculate an inclusive curriculum, representative of the subcultural groups that compose America, will appeal to the diverse audience educated in America today and tomorrow.

Inclusion of Afrocentric perspectives in the communication arts curriculum is one piece of the total multiculturalism curriculum reform picture and, because of the nature of race relations in the United States, it is one of the more controversial aspects. Again, it is understood that in the larger multiculturalism picture, communication arts is but one of the many disciplines slated for modification and the Afrocentric view is but one of the subcultural views to be included in curriculum reform.

A review of literature on the subject of curriculum development and multicultural inclusiveness reveals little that deals with models for curricular development specifically in communication arts. However, much has been written on curriculum development and multicultural inclusiveness that can be applied in communication arts and other disciplines within the social sciences. Helle Bering-Jensen (1990) recommends inclusion of minority contributions in classroom content as a means of supplementing Eurocentric perspectives. Beverly Tatum (1992) offers strategies for overcoming student resistance to race-related content. Emphasis on inclusion of culturally diverse works of literature is described in Pfordresher (1992) and Post (1992). Michael Harris (1992) suggests one means of addressing racial problems is to promote inclusion of African and African-American content in U.S. public schools. Kerry Feldman (1992) emphasizes how anthropology departments can be helpful in choosing multicultural education components. Jerry Gaff (1992) claims that multiculturalism has won the war against Eurocentrism and that we should move to the next step of creating inclusive programs that are educationally valuable.

These views obviously point to the goal of an expanded curriculum.

I approached my research on African-American scholarship as an opportunity to substantively augment my academic orientation. One could merely use a recipe approach of "just add African-American readings and stir" but this would allow only for cosmetic changes. Rather, I approached this as I did my graduate school years. Knowledge learned was intended to become part of my theoretical fabric. Such an approach takes time and thorough analysis. My graduate training was a long in-depth period of study. Any serious modifications of that foundation should come through a similar path.

The communication arts discipline covers a wide range of subject areas including public speaking, interpersonal communication, organizational communication, mass media, rhetoric, journalism, public relations, broadcasting, theater, and cross-cultural studies. I have focused on five courses I teach: rhetorical communication theory, mass media in America, persuasion, communication in the organization, and unity in diversity. A majority of the works are most appropriate in the unity in diversity course.

I used a variety of key words to search for information relevant to communication arts in the Moorland-Spingarn Research Center. The seven most useful key words were rhetoric, communication, narration, persuasion, political oratory, nonverbal communication, and interpersonal relations. The following lists, in parentheses, the number of relevant titles found under each key word heading: rhetoric (36), communication (75), narration (71), persuasion (6), political oratory (7), nonverbal communication (17), and interpersonal relations (35). I reviewed these 247 titles and other relevant materials located in the Moorland-Spingarn Research Center.

I should acknowledge that the communication arts curriculum covers a wide range of subject areas. I recognized that the aforementioned seven key words offer general headings under which other communication arts subject areas are included. For instance, the key word communication includes such sub-areas as organizational communication, group communication, mass communication, cross-cultural communication and sub-specialties within these sub-areas. For instance, mass communication includes new communication technologies and television production. The Center includes all these areas under communication.

Representative works reviewed in this process include *African Culture: The Rhythms of Unity* (Asante and Asante 1990), *Kemet, Afrocentricity and Knowledge Knowledge* (Asante 1990), *The Anatomy of Black Rhetoric* (Payne 1982), *A Comparative Study of Two Approaches for Analyzing Black Discourse* (Phillips 1983), *Rhetoric of Racial Hope* (Hill 1976), *Handbook of Intercultural Communication* (Asante, Newmark, and Blake 1979), *Black Communication* (Mullen 1982), *From Behind the Black Veil: A Study of African-American Narrative* (Stepto, 1979*), Transracial Communication (*Smith 1973), *Cont-*

emporary Black Thought (Asante and Vandi 1980), *Language, Communication, and Rhetoric in Black America* (Smith 1972), and *Afrocentricity* (Asante 1989).

The search for Afrocentric perspectives on human communication, that can be used in courses in the communication arts curriculum, is hindered by obstacles. Most notable is that a vast majority of the works I studied focus on the plight and victimization of African-Americans, Afrocentrism, and lobbying for better treatment of African-Americans. There is an abundance of rich material that can be analyzed as case studies using communication theories for such case study interpretation, but the problem rests on finding communication theories unique to African- American perspectives.

I sought communication theories, authored by African-American scholars, that are theoretically central to my courses. For example, in the interpersonal communication course, descriptions of African-American interpersonal communication can be used for case study analysis but these descriptions do not necessarily equate with being well-grounded theoretical perspectives themselves.

Another problem is that one cannot be sure if the author of a book or journal article is African-American. Even though the Moorland-Spingarn Research Center is a library of African and African-American scholarship it also has material by authors of other races. For example, Harry Triandis is included in the Moorland-Spingarn Research Center. Thus, I assumed Triandis was African-American until I met his daughter, who conveyed he is not African-American. She said many people assume he is African-American because of his research.

A related question is "can a non-African-American be a credible scholar on African-American perspectives?" Would a native of Kenya (who came to the United States as an adult scholar) have greater license in understanding the African-American perspective than a European-American born and raised in Harlem? What distinctions are there in this regard and how are they constructed?

I find this to be a relevant line of questioning in that some native African-Americans, born and raised in the United States, have been labeled as not being "authentic" African-Americans (i.e., Shelby Steele, author of *By the Content of Our Character*, and U.S. Supreme Court Judge Clarence Thomas). Are there "imitation" African-Americans among us? What is the litmus test for such a distinction? Should their writings not be regarded as African-American scholarship? On one visit at Howard University, while wrestling with these questions, I encountered a library reference clerk who was wearing a sweatshirt that proclaimed, "It's a black thing. You wouldn't understand." The confusion regarding who can be an authentic African-American scholar seems to be commensurate with the sweatshirt's message.

Conveying African-American perspectives in the classroom poses a sensitive lecturing issue. Particularly, how far should an instructor go in acknowledging authorship of a particular viewpoint as being African-American? I sat in on a lecture where the instructor clarified authorship of a perspective as African-American and some African-American students found acknowledgment of the African-American source to be patronizing. The larger issue becomes "should the ethnic/racial background of all theorists be acknowledged?" This could become an invasion of privacy at some point.

Another classroom issue deals with evolving language norms regarding how racial groups are labeled. For instance, one student sparked heated discussion when she said she was confused by the label "people of color." Her point: It is a senseless expression, because 1) white is a color, thus everybody is a person of color, and 2) what is the difference between "colored person" and a "person of color"? This was followed up by the statement African-Americans do not like to be called "colored people," which was rebutted with "Why does the leading organization of African-Americans, who don't like to be called 'colored people,' have their organization titled National Association for the Advancement of Colored People?" These classroom issues are relevant because the reason I am searching for Afrocentric perspectives on human communication is so I can convey them in the classroom, as well as in my research.

In this study of African-American communication arts scholars, the most prominent name I found was Molefi Asante, who is arguably one of the most important writers regarding the African-American perspective. On the May 12, 1993, showing of ABC's "*Nightline,*" Asante was interviewed by Ted Koppel regarding the content and legitimacy of the African-American perspective. He was a keynote speaker at the 1995 annual meeting of the National Communication Association (the primary professional organization in communication studies). Asante is presently the chair of the Black Studies Department at Temple University. Given his stature in and outside of academia, Asante is a scholar who can be studied as a key player in the development of African-American thought. As such, the content of his writings can be viewed as exemplifying the African-American perspective.

Koppel introduced Asante as an important figure in African-American studies and, during the interview, Asante stated "I have written thirty-three books and two hundred articles (in black studies)" (*Nightline*, May 12, 1993). I researched Asante's works at the Moorland-Spingarn Research Center and found twenty-four books listing Asante as author or coauthor (some of these books are listed under the name Arthur L. Smith, his previous name). Of the communications related books, 63 percent are edited books. That is, Asante did not write the books but he did invite other authors to write chapters in the books. Seventy-one percent of these books are coedited with other individuals, and 27 percent of these books are authored soley by Asante.

A review of communications related works, attributed to Asante, sheds light on his perspective. This will be done in chronological order. Under his previous name, Arthur L. Smith, Asante edited *Language, Communication and Rhetoric in Black America* (1972), which describes "communicative experiences of black Americans." He then authored *Transracial Communication* (1973) which analyzes black-white interaction from a black perspective. He coedited the *Handbook of Intercultural Communication* (Asante, Newmark, and Blake 1979), which focuses on intercultural communication dynamics.

Contemporary Black Thought (Asante and Vandi 1980) was coedited by Asante. He wrote three chapters dealing with international and intercultural relations, the "communication person," and television's impact on the language of black children. He also coauthored *A Guide to African and African-American Art* (Asante and Welsh 1980), a forty-page pamphlet describing art linked to the African tradition.

Two books deal specifically with the African tradition: *The Great Zimbabwe: An Ancient African City-State* (Asante 1983), which Asante edited, and *The Rhythms of Unity: A Bibliographic Essay in African Culture* (Asante and Asante 1985), which Asante coedited. Obviously, these two books are related to African-American scholarship in communication arts only in that Africa provides a foundation for African-American thought.

A similarly titled book, *African Culture: The Rhythms of Unity*, coedited by Asante, describes African culture, dance, education, time awareness, socialism, and personality (Asante and Asante 1985). Yet another book with the same title and authors, *African Culture: The Rhythms of Unity* (Asante and Asante 1990), elaborates on the previous book of the same title. This book was preceded by *Afrocentricity* (Asante 1989), a one-hundred page booklet that describes Afrocentric views on science, sociology, black liberation, and oppression. *Kemet, Afrocentricity and Knowledge* (Asante 1990) gives Asante's perspective on the oppression of blacks. His work exemplifies the previously mentioned rich abundance of material, authored by African-American writers, that can be analyzed in case study analysis using communication theories. However, Asante does not offer communication theories or conceptual frameworks unique to African-American perspectives. I have used material, authored by African-Americans that describes their plight, for case study analysis in class and found such applications to work well with a wide range of college audiences. The idea of African-American scholarship and development of African-American studies academic departments has been debated by a variety of sources. Some of these positions will be described to provide representative understanding of the issue.

On the aforementioned *Nightline* segment, Anthony Martin, a black studies professor at Wellsley College, defended why he uses a textbook authored by the Nation of Islam, that says Jews are genetically proned to enslaving others. Martin explained, "I have a right to interpret my history" (*Nightline*, May 12, 1993). On the same show, Dinesh D'Souza, from the American Enterprise Institute, stated black studies departments were founded in the 1960's as a result of political pressure, colleges have let black studies go unchecked, and black studies do not have clear standards for evaluating scholarship (*Nightline*, May 12, 1993).

Leon Jaroff, in an article titled "Teaching Reverse Racism," writes "the afrocentric movement is intended to acquaint U.S. blacks with their long ignored African heritage and raise their self-esteem" (Jaroff 1994, 74). He explains that an African-American perspective taught at Southern Methodist University maintains "all Egyptians were black, and their abundance of the dark skin pigment, melanin, not only made them more humane and superior to lighter-skinned people in body and mind but also provided such paranormal powers as ESP (extrasensory perception) and psychokinesics" (Jaroff 1994, 74).

Mary Lefkowitz, professor of classics at Wellesley College, offers her view of Afrocentric perspectives in a *Chronicle of Higher Education* article titled "Combating False Theories in the Classroom":

> If afrocentric assertions, despite the passion with which they are put forward, cannot be supported by evidence, statistics, or facts, why do such courses remain in the curricula of legitimate colleges and universities? . . .Unfortunately, many colleges and universities today are allowing professors to invoke academic freedom to teach material that until recently would never have appeared in any educational curriculum, much less in a university. Such materials include the absurd propositions, sometimes lumped under afrocentrism, that Europeans are "ice people" who are genetically inferior to the "sun people" of Africa, that Greeks stole their philosophy from Egypt, and that Jews were primarily responsible for the slave trade. Reputable scholars have repeatedly produced evidence that these statements are false, but it has consistently been ignored by afrocentrists. (Lefkowitz 1994, 1).

She supports her assertion with an example of the "afrocentric claim Aristotle stole his philosophy from the Library of Alexandria, which was not built until after Aristotle's death" (Lefkowitz 1994, 1).

In *Campus,* Craig Hymowitz and Alan Sauers state, "Black Studies launched itself not into a serious study of black culture or history, but instead into revisionism—the creation of a culture of victimization and phony historical record with an eye more toward building black self-esteem than uncovering historical fact" (1994, 6). The article is titled "In Search of Self-Esteem: The Corruption of Black Studies."

Other events, less directly related to black studies departments, have hurt the credibility of African-American scholarship. Martin Luther King is perhaps the most widely recognized African-American of the twentieth century. Revelations by *The Journal of American History* (Thelen 1991) and *Chronicle of Higher Education* (Raymond 1991) that King plagiarized parts of his Ph.D. dissertation could possibly smear the credibility of African-American scholars. "King frequently did not credit the sources for words he claimed to be his own. . . .The word, of course, is plagiarism" (Thelen 1991, 14). That Boston University did not revoke King's Ph.D., upon discovering the plagiarism, exemplifies how sensitive this issue is.

Regarding the larger issue of multiculturalism, columnist John Leo blames the City University of New York's decline on multiculturalism. Leo quotes Heather MacDonald as saying "CUNY is at the cutting edge of a nationwide movement to do away with the very distinction between academic proficiency and deficiency and replace it with the concept of competence in one's own culture" (*U.S. News & World Report,* August 15, 1994, 20). Three months later, Leo wrote about an estrangement connected to the rise of multiculturalism. "The shift has to do more with morally dubious moves taking place behind the word 'diversity'. . . . As long as ordinary white male workers are seen through ideological lenses as patriarchal overlords who deserve to be brushed aside, race-and-gender balkanization will accelerate" (*U.S. News & World Report,* November 21, 1994, 3).

In an essay titled "The Search for Virtues," Lance Morrow responds to multiculturalism and its negative effects on societal virtues by describing William Bennet's *The Book of Virtues.* "The American challenge now is not to pay homage to every ethnic sensitivity, but rather to encourage universally accepted ideals of behavior: self-discipline, compassion, responsibility, friendship, work, courage, perseverance, honesty, loyalty and faith" (*Time,* March 7, 1994, 78).

Gary Trudeau's politically oriented comic strip "Doonesbury" featured a ten day series that commented on the shortcomings of multiculturalism. The series begins with a math professor who is complimenting his students on their incorrect guesses in class. He is accused of giving a racist grade of B+ by the recipient who feels disempowered and marginalized because of the grade. The student, a white male, explains his answer may be incorrect to the professor but that his culture teaches the incorrect answer, thus he should receive credit for his answer.

The student goes on to explain that receiving a bogus grade shows professorial disrespect for his community (a Greek-lettered fraternity). The student feels victimized by the low expectations of the professor. The student then initiates a lawsuit against the professor claiming discrimination against the "Greco-American athletic community." The professor, seeking to understand the plight of the student, is told "it's a Greek thing—you wouldn't understand" (Trudeau 1993).

Edwin Delattre comments on multiculturalism: "At Harvard, no undergraduate student is required to study western culture, though most must study a non-western ('foreign') culture in order, as the catalog says, 'to provide fresh perspectives on one's own cultural assumptions and traditions.' There is no mention of assessing, say, the assumptions and traditions of non-western caste systems, non-western institutionalized slavery, non-western political tyranny, and non-western genocide" (Delattre 1990, 22). In a similar vein, Princeton University historian Bernard Lewis writes, "While the phenomenon of slavery is universal, what is distinctively western is the movement for the abolition of slavery" (Lewis 1990, 4).

Shelby Steele, an African-American professor, offers a rejoinder view of the direction higher education should take regarding African-Americans. "What we need now is a new spirit of pragmatism in racial matters where blacks are seen simply as American citizens who deserve complete fairness and in some cases developmental assistance, but in no case special entitlements based on color. . . . The white message to blacks must be: America hurt you badly and that is wrong, but entitlements only prolong the hurt while development overcomes it" (Steele 1990, 91).

Locating Afrocentric perspectives is a goal that must be closely followed by an understanding of how to convey the perspectives in the classroom. I have been a student and/or teacher in higher education since 1973. I have seen attempts from the perspectives of student and teacher. As a college sophomore at a small liberal arts college, I experienced a required course titled "Black Studies." This course was taught to students who did not want to take the course, taught by faculty who did not want to teach it, and kept in the catalog by administrators afraid to drop it. I believe the problem occurred because faculty were assigned to teach the course and had little, if any, input into what was taught. Multiculturalizing the curriculum should be based on ownership by each faculty member. It is difficult to believe a faculty member can be forced to adopt unfamiliar material for application in the classroom and teach it in a competent manner. A more successful approach would create an environment, through the use of incentives, that encourages individual faculty members to discover a variety of cultural perspectives and build upon what they already know.

The idea of ownership can be an effective motivating influence with students as well. Such an approach empowers students to discover and celebrate various cultural perspectives on classroom subject matter. This can be done through class assignments stressing independent research. Independent student research findings, shared in the classroom, can enhance the learning experience of all students in a course and the professor. Thus, lifelong learning occurs for all involved.

The mission statement of the college at which I teach encourages all members of the academic community "to contemplate truth and share with others the fruits of this contemplation." The search for truth is a consistent referent. The findings presented in this chapter are the product of my search for truth. The findings are not meant to be the conclusive last word on the subject. Rather, they are a contribution toward that end.

Note: I would like to acknowledge the Lilly Foundation for the generous grant they provided that supported this study. Dr. Bill Carroll (President, Illinois Benedictine University) was instrumental in helping me to secure this funding. I would like to thank Dr. Jannette Dates (Dean of the College of Communication at Howard University) for mentoring me during my study of aftrocentric perspectives and her hospitality during my visits at Howard University. We have co-authored journal articles as a result of our work together and I have found her to be an excellent resource and guide.

References

Asante, M. K. 1989. *Afrocentricity.* Trenton, NJ: African World Press.
———. 1990. *Kemet, Afrocentricity, and Knowledge.* Trenton: African World Press.
Asante, M. K. and K. Welsh, 1980. *A Guide to African and African-American Art.* Buffalo: Museum of African and African-American Art.
Asante, M. K., ed. 1983. *The Great Zimbabwe: An Ancient African City-State.* New runswick: Transaction Books.
Asante, M. K. and K. W. Asante, eds. 1985. *The Rhythms of Unity: A Bibliographic Essay in African Culture.* Westport, CT: Greenwood Press.
———. 1985. *African Culture: The Rhythms of Unity.* Westport, CT: Greenwood Press.
———. 1990. *African Culture: The Rhythms of Unity.* Trenton, NJ: African World Press.
Asante, M. K., E. Newmark, and C. Blake, eds. 1979. *Handbook of Intercultural Communication.* Beverly Hills: Sage Publishers.
Asante, M. K. and A. S. Vandi, eds. 1980.*Contemporary Black Thought.* Beverly Hills, California: Sage.

Battle, T. C. "Moorland-Spingarn Research Center, Howard University," *Library Quarterly* 58, no. 2, 143-146.

Bering-Jensen, H. 1990. "Teaching All Things to All People," *Insight* 6, issue 14 (April 2): 49-51.

Congressional Record, November 21, 1989.

Delattre, E. J. 1990. "Ethics and the Isms: Elitism, Multiculturalism, Centrisms, Racism, Sexism and Feminism," Olin Public Lecture Series, Boston University (November 26).

Feldman, K. D. 1992. "Multicultural Education and Anthropology: 'The Rise of Civilization' as a Foundation Course," *Human Organization* 51, no. 2, (Summer): 185-186.

Gaff, J. G. 1992. "Beyond Politics," *Change* 24, no. 1 (January): 30-35.

Gomez, M. 1992. "Diversity 101," *Hispanic* 5, no. 9 (October): 50-52.

Gordon, E. W., and M. Bhattacharyya. 1992. "Human Diversity, Cultural Hegemony, and the Integrity the Academic Canon," *Journal of Negro Education* 61, no. 3 (Summer): 405-418.

Harris, M. D. 1992. "Afrocentrism and Curriculum: Concepts, Issues, and Prospects," *Journal of Negro Education* 61, no. 3 (Summer): 301-316.

Hill, R. L. 1976. *Rhetoric of Racial Hope*. Brockport, NY: McDaniel Press.

Hymowitz, C. L. and Sauers, T. A. 1994. "In Search of Self-Esteem: The Corruption of Black Studies," *Campus* (Winter): 6.

Jaroff, L. 1994. "Teaching Reverse Racism," *Time*, 4 April, 74-75.

Lefkowitz, M. 1994. "Combating False Theories in the Classroom," *Chronicle of Higher Education*, 19 January, B1-2.

Leo, J. 1994. "It's the Culture Stupid," *U.S. News & World Report* (21 November), 30.

———. 1994."A University's Sad Decline," *U.S. News & World Report* (15 August), 20.

Lewis, B. 1990. "Christianity and Slavery," *Crisis* (November): 4.

Morrow, L. 1994. "The Search for Virtues," *Time*, 7 March, 78.

Mullen, R. 1982. *Black Communication*. Lanham, MD: University Press of America.

Nightline. 1993. American Broadcasting Corporation, 12 May 1993.

Payne, J. C 1982. *The Anatomy of Black Rhetoric*. Tallahassee, FL: Graphic Communications Associates.

Pfordresher, J. 1992. "Better and Different Literature in Our Time," *Design for Arts in Education* 93, no. 4, (March): 2-10.

Phillips, L. C 1983. *"A Comparative Study of Two Approaches for Analyzing Black Discourse." Ph.D. Dissertation*. Howard University.

Post, D. 1992. "Through Joshua Gap: Curricular Control and the Constructed Community," *Teachers College Record* 93, no. 4 (Summer): 673-696.

Raymond, C. 1991. "Allegations of Plagiarism Alter Historians' Views of Civil-Rights Leader," *Chronicle of Higher Education* (10 July), A5.

Smith, A. L. 1973. *Transracial Communication*. Englewood Cliffs, NJ: Prentice-Hall.

———, ed. 1972. *Language, Communication, and Rhetoric in Black America*. New York: Harper and Row.

Steele, S. 1990. *The Content of Our Character*. New York: HarperCollins Publishers.

Stepto, R. B. 1979. *From Behind the Veil: A Study of African-American Narrative*. Chicago: University of Illinois Press.

Tatum, B. D. 1992. "Talking About Race, Learning About Racism: The Application of Racial Identity Development Theory in the Classroom," *Harvard Educational Review* 62, no. 1 (February): 1-24.

The Arthur B. Spingarn Collection of Negro Authors. n.d. Washington D.C.: Moorland Foundation, Howard University Library(ca. 1947).

Thelen, D. 1991. "Becoming Martin Luther King, Jr.: An Introduction," *The Journal of American History* (June): 11-22.

Trudeau, G. "Doonesbury" cartoon series, syndicated, 20-31 December 1993.

Viadero, D. 1992. "Issue of Multiculturalism Dominates Standards Debate," *Education Week* 11, no. 31 (22 April): 18.

Williams, M. A. 1990. *Blacks and the Media: Communication Research Since 1978.* Washington, D.C.: Howard University.

Part Two

Qualitative Interpretation Case Studies

Chapter Nine

The Symbolic Interactionist Use of Participant Observation: A Study of Conflict Resolution Communication in a Counter-Cultural Setting

This chapter will explain the symbolic interactionist use of participant observation. It will clarify the meanings of, and relationship between, symbolic interaction and participant observation. I will describe a study that employed the participant observation method within a symbolic interactionist framework, to exemplify the application of this approach. This study examines conflict resolution communication in a countercultural setting.

The symbolic interactionist framework is a commonly accepted perspective from which to study communication. In "Communication as Symbolic Interaction: A Synthesis," Nwanko describes the communicative process as "symbolic interaction in which two symbolic systems (persons or groups) interact by use of significant symbols" (Nwanko 1973).

Gronbeck outlines a variety of research methods that a communication analyst may employ within the symbolic interactionist framework.

> The participant observation techniques allow researchers to dig deeply and systematically into "texts"; the fantasy theme methodology bids the specification of sources of wholesale cultural mythoi and visions; Burkean concepts explicate the ways in which human motives are encoded and lived out in messages; and, the macroscopic investigations of interpersonal constructions, their ritualizations and expressions, lead steadily toward a "grand theory" of society as formed, enacted, and regulated by communication/rhetorical processes. (Gronbeck 1980)

My position advocates the symbolic interactionist use of participant observation and stresses the importance of the "texts" that are studied.

The participant observer seeks to understand the view of the world as perceived by the subjects being studied. "Essentially, the researcher 'brackets' his own assumptions to see how the subjects of the investigation themselves view everyday life situations" (Hickson 1983). Beach emphasizes the "study of social order within naturally occurring events. Particular attention is drawn to how everyday activities are routinely accomplished according to the rules, maxims, and strategies that practical reasoners use to organize communication" (Beach 1982).

Participant observation provides a unique insight into a research problem. "Notwithstanding, participant observation has extremely great potential for communication research, because it can give the researcher detailed knowledge of communication processes in context" (Poole 1982). The researcher is able to observe specific events and is also able to observe previous and following occurrences.

Gerry Philipsen used participant observation in "Speaking 'Like a Man' in Teamsterville." He was interested in finding what groups in the United States view speaking as an effective means of social influence. Philipsen states there is a lack of information in this area and this deficit "should be remedied by descriptive and comparative studies of American speech communities" (Philipsen 1975). In a similar study, Thurmon Garner used participant observation to analyze obscene folkloric speech events, popularly known in black communities as "playing the dozens," in "Playing the Dozens: Folklore as Strategies for Living" (Garner 1983).

Statement of Problem

The problem of this study dealt with conflict resolution communication attempts practiced by the Woodstock Food Cooperative. (Pseudonyms are used in the place of real names of individuals and organizations discussed in this study.) I sought to find if the primary ideals of the counterculture were evidenced in the communication attempts at conflict resolution.

Analysis was highlighted through comparison and contrast with another organization. The organization, Sigma Tau Omega Fraternity, represented an opposite position on the philosophical continuum (using counterculture as one end of the continuum and dominant culture as the other end). The co-op presented itself as based on counterculture philosophy and Sigma Tau Omega presented itself as based on dominant culture philosophy.

The co-op and Sigma Tau Omega represented two ends on the counterculture-dominant culture continuum. I hypothesized there would be differing communication attempts to conflict resolution within each organization. Furthermore, the different communication attempts would reflect their cultural base. Analysis of these attempts was focused on formal settings (meetings) and informal settings (outside of meetings). Regarding formal settings, I hypothesized different conflict resolution communication attempts would be based on the consensus principle (everyone must agree) practiced by the co-op and the "majority rules" principle practiced by Sigma Tau Omega. With informal settings, I hypothesized different conflict resolution communication attempts would be based on the egalitarian (all members have equal power) principle practiced by the co-op and the hierarchy principle practiced by Sigma Tau Omega. The hierarchy within Sigma Tau Omega was based on pin number (indicating seniority), role as a fraternity officer, and physical size of the member.

Consideration of Method

Symbolic Interactionism

Three primary sociological approaches to the study of human behavior are functionalist, conflict, and interactionist. The functionalist perspective, led by Durkheim, views society as a structure of interrelated parts. The conflict perspective, influenced strongly by Marx, sees social change as evolving from conflict between the social classes. The interactionist perspective, emphasized by Mead, is concerned with the social interactions of everyday life (Robertson 1977).

Early interactionism was based on symbolic behavior, the interpretive element, and the notion of emergence. The genesis of symbolic interactionism can be seen through the work of five people: James, Cooley, Dewey, Thomas, and Mead. James, a pragmatist, stressed habit, instinct, and self. Cooley, from the Chicago school, utilized sympathetic introspection: we should understand the meanings and interpretations of the actor. Dewey, also from the Chicago school, emphasized the phylogenetic framework; human behavior is different in degree, rather than in kind. Thomas felt that human behavior methods should tap the values and attitudes of the actor. Mead, from the Chicago school, is recognized as the father of symbolic interactionism. In *Mind, Self, and Society*, he states that organisms are viewed in relation to their environment and the environment is determined by the sensitivity of the organism (Meltzer, Petras, and Reynolds 1977, 1-40).

There are four main schools of thought within symbolic interactionism: the Chicago, Iowa, Dramaturgical, and Ethnomethodological schools. The Chicago school, led by the theories of Blumer, is based on a qualitative and humanistic approach: the world should be viewed "through the eyes of the actor." Blumer sees human behavior as unpredictable and indeterminate. The self is composed of the "I" and the "me." Within this framework the "I" is impulsive and the "me" is a collection of organized attitudes. Perceptions are initially received through the "I" and then are filtered through the "me." Blumer's image of human behavior dictates his method (Meltzer et al. 1977, 55-67).

The Iowa school, led by the theories of Kuhn, is based on a quantitative and scientific approach. Kuhn believes that symbolic interactionism can be empirically measured and operationalized. He sees human behavior as being role played. As opposed to Blumer, he views the self as being comprised only of the "me." Kuhn's method dictates his image of human behavior (Meltzer et al. 1977, 55-67).

The comparison of approaches purported by Blumer and Kuhn is clarified through Littlejohn's discussion of the foundations of symbolic interactionism.

> While Blumer strongly criticizes the trend in the behavioral sciences to operationalize, Kuhn makes a special point to do just that! As a result, Kuhn's work moves much more toward microscopic analysis than does the traditional Chicago approach. In other words, Kuhn prescribes the very methods which Blumer dislikes—a) adhering to scientific method protocol, b) engaging in replication of research studies, c) relying on the testing of research hypothesis, and d) employing so-called operational procedures. (Littlejohn 1977)

By using a qualitative and humanistic approach, Blumer's method is more sensitive to flexibility if his image of the observed human behavior dictates such a need. Kuhn's use of a quantitative and scientific approach results in a method that is less sensitive to change.

The Dramaturgical school, led by the theories of Goffman, purports that social interaction is based on the management of the impressions we receive from each other. We "put on a show" for each other as a way of conveying meaning. This perspective is evidenced in Goffman books, such as *The Presentation of Self in Everyday Life* (1959), *Interaction Ritual* (1967), and *Encounters* (1961).

The Ethomethodological school, led by the theories of Garfinkel, studies the rational properties of indexical expressions as ongoing accomplishments and occurrences in everyday life. Lauer and Handel broaden the perspective by describing it as the study of folk methods for deciding on questions of fact (Lauer and Handel, 1977).

The four main schools of thought within symbolic interactionism engulf various theoretical and methodological positions regarding the understanding and study of human behavior. Although there is variety, Blumer has presented a common theoretical thread that runs through the four schools of symbolic interactionist thought.

Blumer coined the term symbolic interactionism. He explains three premises of symbolic interactionism that define its basic tenets and are accepted in all areas of the field:

The first premise is that human beings act toward things on the basis of the meanings that the things have for them. . . . The second premise is that the meaning of such things is derived from, or arises out of, the social interaction that one has with one's fellows. . . . The third premise is that these meanings are handled in, and modified through, an interpretive process used by the person in dealing with the things he encounters. (Blumer 1969)

Meanings are viewed as social products: stimulation, interpretation, and response. This process can vary depending on the circumstances but these three variables will always be present. The symbolic interactionist can engage in critical analysis by seeking to recognize these three phenomena.

The wide perspective provided by symbolic interactionism can be appreciated when one considers the difference between the Chicago and Iowa schools. The arguments and positions maintained by these schools engulf the qualitative and quantitative approaches. On the one side, Blumer advocates the qualitative approach through the use of participant observation, so the researcher can understand the view of the actor's world through the actor's eyes. On the other side, Kuhn advocates the quantitative approach through the use of empirical measurement and operationalism. The Who Am I Test, constructed by Kuhn, is an example of such an attempt (Meltzer et al. 1977, 55-67).

I chose a qualitative and humanistic approach, as outlined through Blumer's three basic premises, as the most beneficial for this study. Such an approach allows for, what Howard S. Becker underlines as, "rich experiential context" of observation of the event and observation of previous and following events (Filstead 1970, 141).

Gerald Miller discusses similar considerations in "Laboratory Versus Field Approaches to the Study of Communication and Conflict." He limits his discussion to ways in which both approaches complement each other.

The collection of descriptive data enhances our understanding of some of the dimensions of "real-world" social conflict. . . . Field research can also aide in the identification of significant constructs, a task to which I have already assigned high priority. By observing communication and social conflict in natural settings, an ingenious person may inductively arrive at new category systems, or new classes of variables. . . . Laboratory settings allow the researcher to construct the environment that he wishes to study, and they enable him to manipulate independent variables more unambiguously. (Miller 1974, 218)

Using a more abstract style, Miller metaphorically describes the complementary roles played by laboratory and field research:

But before one can embark on . . . a journey,hemust choose a conveyance. The laboratory and the field represent two vehicles available to our traveler. To carry the analogy a step further, the laboratorycanbelikened to a private limousineand field to public transportation. In the cloistered confines of the former, the researchercanpartially create an environmentto study and to manipulate; if he wants arear-seat bar or a private telephone, he may install them; if he tires of them, he may have them removed. The disadvantage, of course, is that he may lose touch with what is going on outside the curtained windows. In the din and clamor of the latter, the researcher's fellow travelers often jostle him with such bewildering confusion and rapidity that he becomes uncertain whether he is approaching his stop, or whether he has, in fact, passed it. Still,if he can keep his wits together, he can derive satisfaction from the knowledge that his ride has exposed him to a glimpse of reality not readily accessible to the limousine passenger. (Jandt 1973, xiii-xiv)

The symbolic interactionist perspective allows research from the qualitative and quantitative approaches. It is usually associated with qualitative research but it can easily be applied with quantitative methodology. The decision regarding how to use the symoblic interactionist perspective should be based on the specific needs of the situations studied. As previously mentioned, Blumer advocates the qualitative approach through the use of participant observation, so the researcher can work to better understand the view of the actor's world through the actor's eyes. From the other view, Kuhn advocates the quantitative approach through the use of empirical measurement and operationalism (Melzer et al. 1977, 55-60).

I utilized the qualitative approach, emphasized by Blumer, and based my decision on the specific needs of the situations studied. I also used the dramaturgical perspective, emphasized by Goffman, for analysis of the research problem.

Understanding Communication Through Symbolic Interactionism

One can gain a clear understanding of the concept of communication through the framework offered by the premises of symbolic interactionism. That is, day-to-day communication can be readily interpreted through the symbolic interactionist perspective.

As previously discussed, symbolic interactionism provides a wide perspective for the observation of human behavior. In fact symbolic interactionism is one of the broadest overviews of the role of communication in society. It influences many areas of communication theory, including role theory, reference group theory, social perception and person perception, self theory, interpersonal theory, and language and culture (Kuhn 1964). This wide applicability can be seen as a strength (it has many applications) or weakness (it is somewhat diluted because it has such a broad base).

Manis and Meltzer (1972) provide six basic propositions of symbolic interaction. First, the mind, self, and society are processes of personal and interpersonal interaction. Second, language is the primary mechanism in the development of the individual's mind and self. Third, mind is the internalization of social processes in the individual. Fourth, behaviors are constructed by the person on the course of acting. Fifth, definition of the situation by the actor is the primary means for human conduct. Sixth, the self is comprised of societal definitions as well as unique definitions.

Littlejohn emphasizes "the need to study the individual in relation to the social situation. . . the person cannot be studied apart from the setting in which behavior occurs" (1977, 85). To achieve this need "the goal of the researcher must be to empathize with the subject, to enter his realm of experience, and to attempt to understand the unique value of the person" (Littlejohn 1977, 85).

The "definition of the situation" is stressed as one of Manis and Meltzer's basic propositions of symbolic interaction. Faules and Alexander develop this proposition and explain its ramifications.

> The symbolic interactionist defines the naming or labeling of the things being perceived as "definition of the situation." The implication as defining situations is broader and more communicative than merely labeling the perception; "definition of a situation" locates the process of observing an event and then finding symbols to communicate the event. Thus defining situations implies that events are symbolized so that they may be explained to others, and indeed this is the process of informing. (1978, 167)

During the informing process there is an exchange of information between, or among, the individuals. "Information may be defined as the report of personal perceptions and of social realities that are exchanged between people. Communication is the method most often used to exchange or collect information, because people rely on symbols to link themselves with other people" (Faules and Alexander 1978, 168).

Faules and Alexander highlight this process by acknowledging other exchanges that are accomplished. "The communication process should reveal an individual's lines of conduct and self-conception" (Faules and Alexander 1978, 246). "The basic 'stuff' of communication is content. . . . The way in which those basic ideas are communicated defines the relationship between the communicators. In other words, communication simultaneously offers both content and relationship" (Watzlawick et. al. 1967, 33).

From this discussion, the relationship between symbolic interactionism and communication can be better understood. Communication is central to symbolic interaction. "To the symbolic interactionist, communication is at the heart of human action" (Faules and Alexander 1978, 143). It is through communication that we come to understand symbolic interaction. Similarly, symbolic interactionism provides a base from which we can interpret communication (Littlejohn 1977, 91).

My research problem involved analysis of conflict resolution communication attempts. I was able to study the content of conflict and the relationship of those involved by observing their communication, as communication offers both content and relationship. Such observations were collected through a participant observation framework. "The student of human conduct . . . must get inside the actor's world and must see the world as the actor sees it, for the actor's behavior takes place on the basis of his/her own particular meanings" (Meltzer et al. 1977, 57-58).

Conflict resolution is a "process of communication and exchange" (Himes 1980). An inquiry into communication and conflict must give fundamental consideration for the context within which the conflict takes place. Participant observation allows for what Howard S. Becker underlines as "rich experiential context" of observation of the event and observation of previous and following events" (Filstead 1970, 224).

Participant Observation

There are two primary research bases in the social science, qualitative and quantitative. Qualitative research affords an in-depth, detailed, descriptive account of social actions occurring at a specific time and place. Quantitative research usually involves statistical measurements of various kinds that are cross tabulated with one another to explain the variability of a social event" (Johnson 1975, x).

Within qualitative research, participant observation and field research refer to a manner of conducting a scientific investigation where the observer maintains a face-to-face involvement with a particular social setting. A field researcher is one who participates with a group of people in order to observe their everyday actions in their natural social settings (Johnson 1975, ix-x). Over time this allows the field researcher to observe uninhibited behavior, watch for consistencies in this behavior, and draw inferences.

Labovitz and Hagedorn acknowledge five disadvantages and five advantages of participant observation. It is beneficial to recognize these strengths and weaknesses so the researcher can work to strengthen the weak areas and capitalize on the strong areas as much as possible.

The five disadvantages: 1) there is a lack of reliability resulting from random observations; 2) the researcher may sensitize subjects by his presence; 3) the actual role taken by the observer narrows his range of experience; 4) the researcher may become so involved in the group that he loses his objectivity; and 5) the researcher must wait passively for occurrences. The five advantages: 1) the observations take place in a "natural" setting; 2) the researcher is able to observe the emotional reactions of his subjects; 3) a great deal of information can be obtained; 4) the researcher is able to record the context in which observations occur; and 5) if the researcher can establish rapport, he may be able to ask sensitive questions that wouldn't otherwise be possible (Labovitz and Hagedorn 1971, 56-57).

The wide range of areas investigated through participant observation poses the need for basic ideals that field researchers can strive to abide by. With regard to methodology, Liebow quotes Hylan Lewis on the scientific method in relation to participant observation: "The scientific method is doing one's darndest with his brains, no holds barred" (1971, 235).

Junker takes this one step further by emphasizing the "percept to concept" approach. In this manner observation, recording, and reporting should insure that the researcher has the opportunity to relate insightful experience to theoretical analysis, back and forth—weaving the fabric of knowledge (Junker 1960, 13).

Liebow closes his study of street corner men by offering an encompassing comment on the participant observation approach. "In retrospect, it seems as if the degree to which one becomes a participant is as much a matter of perceiving oneself as a participant as it is of being accepted as a participant by others" (Liebow 1967, 256).

Application of Method

Participant observation was the primary method of data gathering. I had two periods of contact with the Woodstock countercultural community. The first was a seventeen-month period between 1979 and 1981 in which I lived in the community and participated with the co-op as a member. The second period, between March 1981 and March 1982, was spent doing fieldwork research in the Woodstock community and particularly at the Woodstock Food Co-op.

I had two periods of contact with Sigma Tau Omega Fraternity. The first was a ten-month period between 1980 and 1981 in which I lived with them as their resident supervisor. As resident supervisor, my duties involved serving as a liaison between the fraternity and the city of Woodstock and Midwestern State University. The second period, between March 1981 and March 1982, was spent doing fieldwork research within the fraternity. I continued to serve as resident supervisor throughout the period of the study.

Zelditch classifies field methods into three broad classes that he defines as being primary:

> **Type I**. Participant Observation. The fieldworker observes and also participates in the same sense that he has durable social relations in the social system. . . .
>
> **Type II**. Informant Interviewing. We prefer a more restricted definition of the informant than most fieldworkers use, namely that he be called an "informant" only where he is reporting information presumed to be factually correct about others rather than about himself. . . .
>
> **Type III**. Enumeration and Samples. This includes surveys and direct, repeated, countable observations. (Filstead 1970, 220)

Data were gathered through participant observation, informative interviews, three surveys, and a review of literature written by or about the organizations. The surrounding community was also focused on for context.

As a member of the co-op, I had direct access to a variety of organizational situations. Access to the co-op was exercised in five areas: general business meetings, working at the co-op, working on three committees, involvement with co-op related social functions, and informally "hanging out" at the co-op. Interviews were conducted with members, and former members, of the co-op. I sought to interview individuals who represented the variety of positions and perspectives maintained by the co-op membership.

Two surveys were used in the gathering of data. I administered a survey that involved processes in formal and informal settings, and the co-op Orientation Committee (of which I was a member) administered a survey regarding the management of the co-op. The co-op printed monthly newsletters, handouts, submitted articles to the FORC newspaper and had articles written about it in the Woodstock area newspapers. I reviewed this literature for information related to the research problem.

Peacock (1968) discusses the use of a second observer in field research settings. I utilized the observations of a second observer to compare and contrast against my own observations.

As resident supervisor of the fraternity, I had access to a variety of organizational situations. I was not a Sig Tau, but I was able to participate in practically all functions within the chapter, excluding ritual initiation of new members. Such involvement included chapter meetings, individual committee meetings, meals, social events, informal recreation, and other day-to-day aspects of fraternity life.

Interviews were conducted with members, and former members, of the fraternity. I sought to interview individuals who were representative of the fraternity membership. I administered a survey that involved processes in formal and informal settings. Sigma Tau Omega published alumni newsletters and handouts, submitted articles to the national fraternity magazine (*Spectrum*), and had articles written about it in the Woodstock area newspapers. I reviewed this literature for information related to the research problem.

Analysis of conflict resolution communication attempts was divided between formal settings (meetings) and informal settings (outside of meetings). Althoughthe study was concerned primarily with conflict resolution communication attempts, I analyzed the lifestyles and value structures of the co-op and fraternity memberships to provide additional perspective for the findings.

Before entering the field, I divided the period of study into four quarters and planned to use each quarter for emphasis on different aspects of research. This approach provided me with a rough timetable within which I gauged my research efforts. I suggest it as an approach for future field research efforts.

- First quarter: introduce self and intentions to the organization, collect observations relating to the research problem and the overall setting, and collect any written literature written by or about the organizations.
- Second quarter: continue first quarter procedures, be watching for possible interviewees, and possibly begin interviewing.
- Third quarter: conduct interviews to compare and contrast interviewees perceptions with perceptions of the researcher.
- Fourth quarter: conduct surveys to compare and contrast surveyed perceptions with perceptions of the researcher.

The participant observation method has been used to study a variety of research problems and situations. Such a method requires the researcher to be aware of the accuracy of his or her observations and the replicability of his or her methods.

Validity and Reliability

Participant observation, as does any human research method, poses possible problems with validity and reliability. "The problem of validity in field research concerns the difficulty of gaining accurate or true impressions of the phenomena under study. The companion problem of reliability centers on the replicability of observations" (Shaffir, Stebbins and Turowitz 1980, 11-12). Deutscher presents a similar understanding.

> Following the customary distinction, the concept of validity addresses itself to the
> truth of an assertion that is made about something in the empirical world. The
> concept of reliability, on the other hand, concentrates on the degree of consistency
> in the observations obtained from the devices we employ: interviews, schedules,
> tests, documents, observers, informants. (Filstead 1970, 202)

Zeller and Carmines provide further analysis of reliability of empirical
measurements. A reliable measure is one that is repeatable and consistent,
whereas an unreliable measure provides results that are unrepeatable and
inconsistent (Zeller and Carmines 1980).

The ramifications of validity and reliability can be further detailed through
integration of concepts. Best states, "A test may be reliable, even though it is not
valid. A valid test is always reliable" (Best 1977, 190). In "Problems of
Inference and Proof in Participant Observation," Becker emphasizes "the
researcher faces the problem of how to analyze it (data) systematically and then
to present his conclusions so as to convince other scientists of their validity"
(Filstead 1970, 189).

Riley correlates problems of reliability and validity in her discussion of
Whyte's *Streetcorner Society*. Riley examines the implications of personality,
role, and influence.

> Especially in small social systems, introducing not only another person but also
> anotherrole—that ofobserver—can affect markedly the relationships among the
> other members. Thus the researcher, often unintentionally and even unwittingly,
> controls, or changes to some extent the action he is observing.
> Although Whyte made a conscious effort to avoid influencing the actions of the
> group, the effect of his presence is shown in Doc's comment to him: "You've
> slowed me up plenty since you've been down here. Now when I do something I
> have to think what Bill Whyte would want to know about it." (Riley 1963, 291)

Reliability and validity have implicatons far beyond personality, role and
influence. McCall and Simmons view problems of reliability and validity as
falling into three main categories:

> 1) reactive effects of the observer's presence or activities on the phenomena being
> observed,
> 2) distorting effects of selective perception and interpretation on the observer's
> part, and
> 3) limitations on the observer's ability to witness all relevant aspects of the in
> question. (1969, 78)

Regardless of the method of research, there is always a variability of human behavior that will affect research findings. An organization will not remain the same organization from year to year. It will gain and lose members and it will encounter a variety of experiences, however slight or extreme that will change it. Similarly, the variability among researchers can affect consistency among research findings. Each researcher perceives from a frame of reference that has been constructed by various experiences, unique to each individual.

Recognition of the aforementioned problems, regarding validity and reliability, led me to view these concepts on a continuum rather than in an either/or sense. I acknowledge problems of validity and reliability with the method, just as there are problems of validity and reliability with any method. My approach was to acknowledge these problems and to keep them in mind as I sought to attain high degrees of accuracy and truth.

Concern with theoretical considerations, such as validity and reliability, provide parameters within which participant observers can work. During the first stages of fieldwork I periodically reflected on these considerations as I worked to define my role in the field.

Entering the Field and Establishing Relations

Field researchers encounter an initial "trust" barrier when they enter the field. Researchers often recognize four primary theories of trust in dealing with the trust barrier. Johnson acknowledges these theories as being the exchange theory, individual-morality theory, adoption of membership morality theory, and the psychological need theory (1975, 86-89).

The exchange theory is given consideration by Wax when she poses the question "Why should anybody in this group bother to talk to me?" She believes that there is an exchange between the researcher and the informant. Some of the typical "gifts" offered by the researcher include relieving boredom or loneliness, giving the informant a chance to express a grievance, or giving the informant an opportunity to play the ego-enhancing role of an authority or teacher. Wax (1952) points out that the elderly and unoccupied informant is atypical and his statements must be considered in this light.

The psychological-need theory is closely related to the exchange theory. The essence of this ideal is that the research project should be viewed as fulfilling psychological needs of the group (Johnson 1975, 89).

The individual-morality theory is based on the idea that a person becomes accepted as a participant observer more because of the type of person he turns out to be, in the eyes of the field contacts, than because of what he is researching (Johnson 1975, 87).

The adoption of membership morality theory provides a different approach to the morality ideal. From this perspective, the researcher will enhance his acceptance by adopting the morals and norms practiced by the group being studied (Johnson 1975, 88).

Being a member of the co-op and resident supervisor of the fraternity did not ensure a position of trust within the organizations. Although I recognized aspects of all the aforementioned theories of trust, I found the individual morality theory to be most influential in the establishment of my role as a trustworthy individual and researcher. That is, I was accepted as a participant observer more because of the type of person I turned out to be, in the eyes of my field contacts, than because of what I was researching.

Once the participant observer has established a bond of trust, he or she can then begin to work from a participant observer level. Junker distinguishes between four theoretical social levels from which the participant observer can work.

As a complete participant, the fieldworker is a complete member of the in-group and his observer activities are wholly concealed. The fieldworker's observer activities are not wholly concealed in the participant as observer role, but they are subordinated to participant activities; this level may limit his access to some kinds of information. The observer as participant observes activities that are made public at the outset; this level will further limit his access to more guarded types of information. As a complete observer, activities range from the observer hiding behind a one-way mirror, at one extreme, to his activities being completely public in a special kind of theoretical group where there are "no secrets" (Junker 1960, 35).

I had little trouble gaining access to the organizations as I was a member of the co-op and resident supervisor of the fraternity primarily and a researcher of the organizations secondarily. This approach affected the participant observation level I worked from. Regarding Junker's four social levels of participant observation, I chose the participant-as-observer level. That is, I placed a higher priority on my role as a member/resident supervisor of the organizations than my role as a researcher of the organizations.

The various levels of participant observation have received attention in field study literature. Overt research is highly preferred in most settings and covert research is generally advocated only in settings that are outside of the moral community. Discussion of ethical considerations, regarding overt and covert research, will better clarify the preference for an overt approach.

Ethical Considerations

Participant observation, like politics, can be viewed easily from a positive or negative perspective, depending on who is defining the situation. When does observation become spying? Is it possible for a researcher to not influence the events being observed? Should equal ethical considerations be extended to groups such as Campus Crusade for Christ and the Ku Klux Klan? Who should make such decisions? I believe ethical distinctions should be clarified by all researchers throughout the course of study.

There has been much discussion regarding covert research and other ethical considerations. Fichter and Kolb state that those being studied can be harmed in three basic ways when the study is published: secrets of the organization can be revealed, the privacy of individuals can be violated, and reputations can be harmed (Filstead 1970, 267-268). Fichter and Kolb go on to mention a "free pass" category of research for situations where the organization being studied is outside of the moral community:

> In mid-century it seems probable that men like Hitler and Stalin, organized groups like "Murder Incorporated," and Ku Klux Klan, and some others, have placed themselves outside the moral community and have surrendered the protection of its norms. Thus the social scientist need have no qualms about reporting in full detail the activities of such groups and people. (Filstead 1970, 268)

Becker emphasizes that information can be used by outsiders against those being studied. "Their enemies may make use of the opportunity to embarrass or attack them" (Becker 1970, 86). An example of this would be the use of Vietnamese field studies by military intelligence during the Vietnam War. A partial solution to this problem was offered by Barnes in "Some Ethical Problems in Modern Fieldwork": "One way of protecting informants from the effects of publication is to give them pseudonyms" (Filstead 1970, 246).

I have utilized pseudonyms in the place of real names of those individuals and organizations discussed in the study. It is my concern and responsibility that these individuals and organizations not be affected by my method, analysis, findings or conclusions.

Barnes speculates on the role of the field researcher: "The ethnographer has to define his role, or try to do so, so that he can retain the good will of his informants and of the administration, continue to gain the flow of information essential to his research task, and yet remain true to his own basic values" (Filstead 1970, 240).

Further distinctions, in relation to moral codes, are offered by Erikson:

> But a good deal more is at stake here than the sensitivities of any particular person, and my excuse for dealing with an issue that seems to have so many

subjective overtones is that the use of disguises in social research affects the professional climate in which all of us work and raises a number of methodological questions that should be discussed more widely.

I am assuming here that "personal morality" and "professional ethics" are not the same thing. Personal morality has something to do with the way an individual conducts himself across the range of his human contacts; it is not local to a particular group of persons or to a particular set of occupational interests. Professional ethics, on the other hand, refer to the way a group of associates define their responsibility to one another and to the rest of the social order in which they they work. (Filstead 1970, 253)

By making this assertion Erickson lays the groundwork for a code of behavior that field reserachers should follow. By defining themselves as field researchers he asserts they should abide by commonly held principles inherent in such a profession. Erikson continues this discussion and offers basic guidelines regarding disguised observation:

What I propose, then, at least as a beginning, is the following: first, that it is unethical for a sociologist to deliberately misrepresent his identity for the purpose of entering a private domain to which he is not otherwise eligible; and second that it is unethical for a sociologist to deliberately misrepresent the character of the research in which he is engaged. (Filstead 1970, 259)

Although there are research settings that might ethically dictate a covert approach, I believe long-term participant observation can best be enhanced with an overt approach. Aside from the mutual respect the social scientist owes to society, an overt approach also protects the researcher's self-concept. If one enters the field covertly, and believes oneself to be "spying," then one could easily come to think of oneself as a spy. A covert researcher must always be on guard to protect his or her true motivation for participation with a group. Such an altered self-concept would interfere with the researcher's interactions with those being studied. Thus, the persons being studied would be reacting to a covert researcher, not an overt participant observer. The overt researcher does not need to worry about the participant and researcher extremes that comprise the covert researcher. The overt researcher has a single base to work from, that of overt participant observer.

I represented myself primarily as a "member" of the co-op and secondarily as a "researcher" of the organization. Similarly, I represented myself primarily as the "resident supervisor" of the fraternity and secondarily as a "researcher" of the organization. It was my intent to approach the field overtly. Situational variables dictated the extent and means by which I revealed my secondary (researcher) role. I generally sought to discuss my research interests on a one-to-one basis to enhance clarification of these interests.

Results and Evaluation

After the data collection period, I divided the data into eight quadrants. The quadrants were classified according to different types of conflict resolution communication situations. The eight quadrants were divided, four to each organization, and distinctions were based on formal and informal settings and high and low level controversy issues. Thus, the four quadrants for each organization were high level controversy issues in formal settings, low level controversy issues in formal settings, high level controversy issues in informal settings, and low level controversy issues in informal settings. The findings are based on the consistencies that existed, regarding conflict resolution communication attempts, within each quadrant.

Results of the study indicate co-op conflict resolution communication attempts were based on a counterculture philosophy on the organizational behavior level (i.e., ritual, procedures, clothing styles, jargon, and norms), but the co-op conflict resolution communication attempts were basically the same as the fraternity conflict resolution communication attempts on the core philosophy level. That is, the co-op conflict resolution communication attempts exemplified dominant culture attempts on the core philosophy level.

The formal conflict resolution formats differed, but the power bases were the same. Power was usually based on who had information and position. I found the co-op generally used a form of voting within the consensus process framework, instead of using the actual consensus process. The consensus process was a formal decision-making process whereby all members present must agree on the proposed course of action. Disagreements were to be worked out through discussion and compromise. Theoretically, one member could have veto power over any proposed course of action. The fraternity would simply discuss an issue and then vote on it.

The egalitarian ideals advocated by the co-op were evident on the organizational behavior level, but not on the core philosophy level. Egalitarian ideals were evident within co-op rituals, procedures, clothing styles, jargon, and norms, but the egalitarian ideals were not recognized as genuine on the core philosophy level. The co-op presented itself as egalitarian, but my analysis found consistent behavior contradictory to egalitarian ideals. Informal levels of influence were consistently recognized within the co-op and the fraternity.

The informal hierarchies within the co-op and fraternity affected the conflict resolution communication processes in both formal and informal settings. The fraternity's informal hierarchy was based on the office held within the fraternity, physical size of the member, wit of the member, and the member's pin number. The co-op informal hierarchy was recognized according to the member's ability to be identified with and by other members. Member participation was also recognized as a factor affecting the informal hierarchies of both organizations. That is, participation in the organizations led to enhanced knowledge of the functioning of the organizations and, in turn, led to a position of referent power within the organizations.

The findings can be readily interpreted from the dramaturgical school of symbolic interaction. That is, social interaction is based on the management of impressions we receive from each other. The co-op presented itself as using a consensus process, in formal situations, but analysis found it actually used a form of voting. The co-op presented itself as egalitarian, in informal situations, but analysis found it actually had a recognized hierarchy among the membership. Thus, the co-op presented itself as practicing the countercultural philosophy, but analysis found it actually practiced dominant culture approaches in communication attempts at conflict resolution.

Erving Goffman (1959) develops the dramaturgical ideal in *The Presentation of Self in Everyday Life*:

> I have said that when an individual appears before others his actions will influence the definition of the situation which they come to have. . . . When an individual appears before others he will have many motives for trying to control the impression they receive of the situation. . . . In consequence, when an individual projects a definition of the situation and thereby makes an implicit or explicit claim to be a person of a particular kind he automatically exerts a moral demand upon the others, obliging them to value and treat him in the manner that persons of his kind have a right to expect. (6-13)

The importance of the conflict resolution communication attempts is that the attempts constructed a presentation made by the organization and its members. The conflict resolution communication attempts were a means for the members to convey and affirm their identity through their unique approaches towards conflict.

My goal in writing this report has been to describe and discuss the symbolic interactionist use of participant observation. I have sought to further clarify this approach by applying the theory to a study I undertook which subsequently involved the symbolic interactionist use of participant observation.

The symbolic interactionist use of participant observation, of course, is not limited to studies involving conflict resolution within a counterculture setting.

This approach can be readily applied to a variety of research problems in a variety of settings. Different types of research problems can best be investigated through different types of approaches. It is my hope the symbolic interactionist use of participant observation will be seriously considered as a viable alternative when attempting to study the human being communicating in his or her natural habitat.

References

Beach W. A. 1982. "Everyday Interaction and It's Practical Accomplishment: Progressive Developments in Ethnomethodological Research," *Quarterly Journal of Speech* 68, 314.

Becker, H. S. 1970. *Sociological Work.* Chicago: Aldine Publishing Co.

Best, J. W. 1977. *Research in Education.* NJ: Prentice-Hall.

Blumer, H. 1969. *Symbolic Interactionism.* Englewood Cliffs, NJ: Prentice-Hall.

Faules, D. F., and D. C. Alexander. 1978. *Communication and Social Behavior: A Symbolic Interaction Perspective.* Reading, MA: Addison-Wesley Publishing Co.

Filstead, W. 1970. *Qualitative Methodology.* Chicago: Markham Publishing Co.

Garner, T. 1983. "Playing the Dozens: Folklore as Strategies for Living," *Quarterly Journal of Speech* 69, 47-57.

Goffman, E. 1959. *The Presentation of Self in Everyday Life.* Garden City, NY: Doubleday.

Goffman, E. 1961. *Encounters.* Indianapolis: Bobbs-Merrill.

Goffman, E. 1967. *Interaction Ritual.* Garden City, NY: Anchor Books.

Gronbeck, B. E. 1980. "Dramaturgical Theory and Criticism: The State of the Art (or Science?)," *The Western Journal of Speech Communication* 44, 327.

Hickson, M. 1983. "Ethnomethodology: The Promise of Applied Communication Research?" *The Southern Speech Communication Journal* 48, 186.

Himes, J. S. 1980. *Conflict and Conflict Management.* Athens: University of Georgia Press.

Jandt, F.E. (ed.) 1973. *Conflict Resolution Through Communication.* New York: Harper and Row.

Johnson, J. 1975. *Doing Field Research.* New York: Free Press.

Junker, B. 1960. *Fieldwork: An Introduction to the Social Sciences.* Chicago: University of Chicago Press.

Kuhn, M.H. 1964. "Major Trends in Symbolic Interaction Theory in the Past Twenty-Five Years," *The Sociological Quarterly* 5, 61-84.

Labovitz, S., and Hagedorn, R. 1971. *Introduction to Social Research.* New York: McGraw- Hill Book Co.

Lauer, R., and Handel, W. 1977. *Social Psychology: The Theory and Application of Symbolic Interactionism.* Boston: Houghton-Mifflin Co.

Liebow, E. 1967. *Talley's Corner.* Boston: Little, Brown, and Co.

Littlejohn, S. W. 1977. "Symbolic Interactionism and an Approach to the Study of Human Communication," *Quarterly Journal of Speech* 63, 84-91.

Manis, J. G., and Meltzer, B. N. (Eds.) 1972. *Symbolic Interaction*. Boston: Routledge and Kegan Paul.

McCall, G. J., and J. L. Simons, (Eds.) 1969. *Issues in participant Observation*. Reading, MA: Additon-Wesley.

Meltzer, B.N., J. W. Petras, and L. T. Reynolds, (Eds.) 1977. *Symbolic Interactionism*. Boston: Routledge and Kegan Paul.

Miller, G. R., and H. W. Simons, (Eds.) 1974. *Perspectives on Communication and Conflict*. Englewood Cliffs, NJ: Prentice-Hall.

Nwanko, R. L. 1973. "Communication as Symbolic Interaction: A Synthesis," *Journal of Communication* 23, 207.

Peacock, J. 1968. *Rites of Modernization*. Chicago: The University of Chicago Press.

Philipsen, G. 1975. "Speaking 'Like a Man' in Teamsterville: Culture Patterns of Role Enactment in an Urban Neighborhood," *Quarterly Journal of Speech* 51, 22.

Poole, M. S. "Notes on Observational Methods," Speech Communication Association Convention, Lousiville, Kentucky, 6 November 1982.

Riley, M. W. 1963. *Sociological Research*. New York: Harcourt, Brace, and World Inc.

Robertson, I. 1977. *Sociology*. New York: Worth Publishers.

Shaffir, W. B., R. A. Stebbins, and T. Turowetz, (Eds.) 1980. *Fieldwork Experience: Qualitiative Approaches to Social Research*. New York: St. Martins Press.

Waltzlawick, P., J. H. Beavin, and D. D. Jackson. 1967. *Pragmatics of Human Communication*. New York: Norton, 1967.

Wax, R. 1952. "Reciprocity as a Field Technique," *Human Organization* 11, 34-37.

Zeller, R. A., and E. G. Carmines. 1980. *Measurement in the Social Sciences*. Cambridge: Cambridge University Press.

Chapter Ten

Understanding a Spiritual Youth Camp as a Consciousness-Raising Group: The Effects of a Subculture's Communication

This chapter will describe and analyze a spiritual youth camp that has met one week each summer since it was founded in 1955. The camp began as an outreach ministry of a community church in Columbus, Ohio in 1955, but in 1986 it separated from the church and became an independent entity. It presently is an interdenominational/interracial camp, with more than forty churches represented, that meets at Tar Hollow State Park in southern Ohio (campers come from all over Ohio and surrounding states). I have attended each summer since 1966.

An overall objective of the camp is to provide a setting for the camper (ages are sixth grade through high school graduate) to have a spiritual experience that can serve as a means for greater self-awareness and appreciation for their self potential. The present camp logo is CAMP (Constructing Assured and Motivated People). The event generally includes about 180 campers and forty to fifty staff (counselors, cooks, and support).

No religious denomination is promoted and the religious background of camp participants (campers and staff) is varied. The lack of denominational influence is most likely due to the camp being founded through an outreach ministry of an interdenominational community church. Most sessions usually have a visiting minister for the week but some sessions will have no ministerial staff. Visiting clergy have included religious leaders from a variety of faiths such as Jewish, Catholic, Congregational, Community, Disciples of Christ, Church of Christ, Lutheran, Presbyterian, Methodist and others. It is a common belief that the camp is spiritual but not denominational. The camp directors and founders describe this phenomena as "we want Catholics to go home better Catholics, Presbyterians to go home better Presbyterians, non-Christians to go home better non-Christians, etc."

A goal at the camp is to break down barriers to free self-expression. Since campers are ages 10 to 18, peer pressure influences are particularly strong and can greatly inhibit free expression. Thus, steps are taken to create an environment that rewards genuine sharing and discredits typical peer pressures (i.e., judging others by their clothes, physical appearance, language usage, and racial/ethnic background). Campers typically come to the camp with a set of peer-pressure-oriented norms that staff seek to dilute. The result is usually a normative vacuum that allows more spiritually oriented value norms to evolve.

The means to this end is a collection of activities that consistently celebrate the worth of each individual. Such activities include songs that everyone can sing, periodic use of a "rule of silence" for time to reflect, daily small discussion groups, at least three spiritual services a day (a morning watch, afternoon chapel, and evening vespers), a Thursday night baptism service, a Friday night awards ceremony, the informal evolution of nicknames, emphasis on cabin units (all campers live in a cabin with at least one counselor) and classes (hiking, swimming, sports, and so on).

I have come to define the camp, in academic terms, as a utopian consciousness-raising group. The review of literature reveals little regarding this specific type of camp. This is not surprising given the unique development of the camp. However, a relevant perspective can be constructed by focusing on group camping and consciousness raising groups.

Dickey found "that the effects of camping on an individual often include a positive measurable outcome in terms of self-concept. . . cooperation, ability to deal with stress, and tenacity" (1974, 52-54). Mitchell and Meier see camping as "a unique experience that provides an opportunity for reestablishing our roots, bringing us into harmony with our outdoor heritage, and giving us a perspective beyond that obtained in the narrow confines of a crowded society" (1983, 3). "Organized camping," more specifically, is defined "as being comprised of a community of persons living together as an organized, democratic group in an outdoor setting" (Dimrock 1948, 22-31).

Mitchell and Meier explain "camp life consists of campers and staff who work and live together in small groups" (1983, 4). Such a setting would stress, and benefit by, effective teamwork by participants. "There is probably no better opportunity for complete participation in meeting daily requirements since the camp structure represents a microcosm of a true democratic society. Through this group process campers develop skills in cooperating, sharing, decision making, and assuming leadership and citizenship responsibilities" (Mitchell and Meier 1983, 4).

The benefits of the camp experience are many. Since it is a 24 hour-a-day experience it affects campers in a variety of ways. Some of these benefits include "learning to accept those different than oneself . . . learning that flexibility, sharing, and consideration for others are essential for happy group living . . . reinforcement of good home training . . . developing deep and lasting friendships with both peers and older persons . . . and assisting campers to mature by gradually leading them away from any overdependence on their families" (Mitchell and Meier 1983, 25). There are also benefits to be realized when the camp stresses democratic group living. Mitchell and Meier list seven such lessons: "1) learning how the democratic process works; 2) understanding and accepting camp rules; 3) gaining the courage to take an active part in a meeting and to express honest opinions; 4) learning to abide by the will of the majority while still having concern for the rights and wishes of the minority; 5) learning to get the facts before making a decision; 6) learning to bring problems and disputes out into the open; and 7) gaining experience in problem solving" (1983, 26).

Since the camp environment is a societal microcosm, and is usually removed from society, it offers consciousness-raising opportunities. Chesebro, Cragan, and McCullough define consciousness raising as a "personal face-to-face interaction which appears to create new psychological orientations for those involved in the process" (1973, 136). They say if like-minded people come together to interact on shared religious value structures, communication stages are likely to evolve. There are four such stages:

1) Self-realization of a new identity. This occurs when individuals share their stories as a form of establishing their identity as part of the group.
2) Group identity through polarization. An in-group/out-group recognition is established whereby "non-believers" (those who don't share the beliefs of the group) are acknowledged and the obstacles posed by nonbelieving out-group individuals are described.
3) Establishment of new values by the group. This occurs when the unique values of the in-group are compared to the less desired out-group values and the in-group values are thus reinforced.
4) Relating to other like-minded groups. This includes relating with groups that share the values of the in-group and have similar ways of knowing. (Cragan and Wright 1980, 196-197)

The aforementioned variables related to group camping and consciousness raising are manifested in the following discussion of the camp under study. This description of group camping and consciousness raising provides a framework for understanding the camp.

I first attended the camp in 1966 (during its eleventh year). I learned of it because my family belonged to the church that sponsored the camp. I attended the camp eight years as a camper. This is the maximum number of years an individual can attend as a camper (beginning with the summer after fifth grade and ending the summer after twelfth grade). Since my last year as a camper (1973) I have participated with the camp each year as a counselor. Thus, I have had ample opportunity to observe the camp from the perspectives of camper and counselor. Other than the family that founded the camp, I have attended the camp more than any other participant.

Though the camp is interdenominational, it is strongly rooted in religion. No one denominational perspective is stressed and religious services are generally not led by sanctioned clergy. Spiritual faith is emphasized throughout a typical camp day. Campers participate in a "morning watch" each morning before breakfast. A rule of silence (no talking) is observed during the morning watch. The morning watch offers 10 to 15 minutes of quiet reflection, guided by a one-page handout with thoughts for the day, poetry, and recognition of the camp theme.

A different camp theme is created for each week-long camp session. The theme is woven into the camp activities. Camp themes are also stressed through a camp theme song and are featured on the camp T-shirts distributed to all campers and staff. Past camp themes include "Climb Every Mountain," "Let There Be Peace on Earth (and Let It Begin with Me)," "Reach Out," "Can Do," "Open a New Window, Open a New Door," "When He Calls Me," and "We Are the World."

After morning watch, breakfast is preceded by a prayer, frequently offered by a volunteer camper. Midmorning activities include an hour-long discussion group period that will generally include discussion/reflection regarding spiritual faith. Lunch is preceded with a prayer much like the breakfast prayer. Midafternoon activities include a thirty-minute "chapel" service that usually includes a couple of camp songs, readings (poems, prose, and thoughts) by campers, a main speaker, and a closing prayer. Dinner is preceded with a prayer. There is an early evening "vespers," much like the afternoon chapel, that usually includes camp songs, readings, a main speaker, a performance by the camp choir, and a closing prayer.

A final worship service may occur during the course of the evening, depending on the scheduled evening activities. At a minimum, the camp day will close with a "friendship circle" where all campers and staff form a large circle, sing camp songs, listen to some closing thoughts from the camp directors, and have a closing prayer. When campers return to their cabins for the night, some cabin counselors (or campers) will lead faith-centered discussions or, at times, Bible readings.

Sunday night features a "Never Walk Alone" service in which first-year campers and counselors are escorted, one at a time, by veteran campers, to a large camp fire. The rule of silence is observed and, after a speaker, the camp community sings "You Never Walk Alone." The Thursday night program has two religious services at the lake: a baptism (by immersion in the lake) service, and a late evening vesper service. The final night (Friday) culminates with a communion service, usually held outside, that closes the evening. The rule of silence that is observed during the communion service continues to be observed throughout the night until Saturday morning.

The camp session closes Saturday morning with a friendship circle, songs, and closing prayer. Camp Sunday is celebrated the next day at a church where most camp participants are from, with members of the camp community leading a worship service. (Pseudonyms are used throughout this report.) This service is usually attended by campers, staff, families and camp participants from previous years.

I conducted an interview with the camp codirectors and founders, Rush and Patsy Roberts (husband and wife), during the preparation of this chapter. The interview was done during a late evening "rap session" at camp and focused on their intentions and observations of the camp. The interview was videotaped and I have viewed it many times during my research. This tape includes a number of references to the role of religion at camp.

Rush and Patsy stress the camp can't teach doctrine because there are too many denominations represented amongst the camp community. A general goal is to help all participants to be better people and to respect each other. As stated earlier, they "want Catholics to go home better Catholics, Presbyterians to go home better Presbyterians, non-Christians to go home better non-Christians, etc." In past years, more than forty churches have been represented at the camp but this number dropped off during the late 1970s due to declining church attendance in the United States.

Many of the camp staff are former campers who join the staff after they are too old to attend as campers. Thus, many camp staff have been participating, as campers and staff, for ten to twenty years. When asked "Why do people keep coming back to camp year after year, especially given the diversity of backgrounds represented at camp? What brings us together?" Rush responded, "We each have found a 'spiritual something' at camp . . . and we come back each year looking for it." Patsy broadens the scope of her interpretation in saying "We're all part of a whole . . . a family," to the point that even when they are away from camp, they're still there in spirit.

When Rush speculated on Camp 2025 he expressed his belief that "something will be going on . . . maybe not a weeklong camp as we know it . . . but some type of spiritually-centered group." Thus, religion and a spiritual belief in God (for most people) provide a context for the week at camp.

Related to the spiritual tone of the camp is the utopian atmosphere that is believed to exist and perpetuated by most of the participants. The camp is seen as a retreat from the pressures of American life. Campers and staff come from a wide range of backgrounds and, even with the diversity, participants come looking for "safe-haven" from negative pressures of school, family and trying to understand themselves. Campers share their feelings and consistently console one another in a manner that creates an almost surreal campwide comfort zone. Dedication to the group and respect for the individual is consistently stressed. Thus, although there are conflicts during the course of the week, the camp is frequently referred to as "heaven on earth," "the way things ought to be," and "my favorite week of the year where I can get away from the world." Thus, I recognize the camp as a self-proclaimed utopia.

Rush Roberts acknowledges parents periodically comment that the children they drop-off at camp at the beginning of the week are not the same kids they pickup at the end of the week. Rush says kids "can cry, hug, share, and self-disclose" more in one week than they might during the other fifty-one weeks of the year. The transition from camp to home can be difficult. Patsy mentioned she usually gets sick to her stomach when she leaves camp. Campers tend to be emotional as they leave on Saturday. The previously mentioned Camp Sunday, held at a church the day after camp ends, was developed to help camp participants make the transition from camp to home.

A unique confirmation of camp identities occurs with the Friday night awards ceremony. On Friday afternoon, camp staff deliberate and vote on recipients of the Camper of the Year, Theme Awards (male and female), Most Improved Campers (male and female), and Rookie of the Year (male and female). Campers vote on the Counselor of the Year Award while staff are deliberating. Patsy Roberts and a selected handful of staff select campers who will receive a wide range of other awards that acknowledge camper behavior during the week. The awards ceremony is a very supportive environment with applause and vocal support offered to all award recipients. Not all staff agree with the giving of awards (I have not participated with award deliberations since 1977) but most staff support the custom.

The Roberts family and their management style adds to the unique camp environment. Rush and Patsy founded the camp in 1956 and their children (Rush Jr., Pam, Jan, and Sissy) were active camp participants in their youth and are on the camp staff. Rush and Patsy are the archetypal father and mother of the camp. Their leadership style is authoritarian and, while they consider staff input, they make it clear they make the final decisions. Since the camp separated from a midwestern town community church, and became an independent entity, the camp has been "owned" by Rush and Patsy. If the camp was a society, they would be defined as benevolent dictators.

There have been staff who have quit coming to camp because of disagreements with Rush and Patsy. Given the intense nature of camp, and the variety of interpretations regarding what camp is and should be, the existence of disagreements should be no surprise. I believe such disagreements, and the viewpoints that drive them, actually benefit the camp as invigorating influences. Staff disagreements are telling because their resolution, or lack of resolution, shed light on what the camp philosophy is.

A typical conflict, and typical resolution, occurred when I disagreed with the giving of awards to campers. Rush and Patsy, and most of the staff, strongly support such awards. Resolution evolved when I ceased to participate in that particular activity (meaning I didn't vote in the awards process). Rush and Patsy will generally exercise flexibility to allow individual freedoms without sacrificing benefits to the group.

Some staff have been asked not to return to camp when their contribution to camp is viewed by the Roberts as being detrimental. This is rare however. One atypical scenario shows how a "renegade counselor" was dealt with.

Lamar Shaw was a camper eight years and had been a counselor for ten years when his camp participation was significantly affected. He was very popular with campers but frequently had differences with other counselors. Disagreements tended to deal with Lamar being viewed as too loud and not helping to enforce camp rules. Some viewed him as being disruptive but nobody viewed him as being menacing. He was vocal regarding his opposition to some of the camp programming. Some staff were vocal with opinions they'd like to see him not continue to come to camp. He stayed away one year and referenced his absence as occurring because of his differences with the staff (including Rush and Patsy).

When he returned the year after his absence, he was permitted to come to camp on the condition he would work in the kitchen rather than be a cabin counselor. This limited his interaction with campers significantly. This "exile to the kitchen" was never overtly acknowledged by the Roberts; rather it was described as occurring because the kitchen staff needed help. However, the event sent a clear signal to dissenters that too much overt disagreement could result in an assignment in the kitchen (or, of course, the individual could choose not to return to camp). Although Lamar was assigned to the kitchen, another counselor invited him to sleep in his cabin and colead a daily discussion group.

Having informal influence at camp is a fickle situation. People who have been at camp a long time have influence due to the knowledge they have of the camp and its history. On the other hand, there are individuals who come to camp the first time and within two days are exercising considerable influence on the behavior of others.

I have been friends with the Roberts family all my life. We were members of the same church during my youth. I have never observed Rush or Patsy abuse their power, their work with youth has consistently been referred to as very impressive, but that they have unchecked authority is evident to staff, and staff behavior is subsequently influenced by this. Their dedication to the camp is blatantly evident. They put in many hours to put together a meaningful camp session each year. They are known as leaders who never ask anybody to do anything they wouldn't do themselves.

Their leadership style can best be described as "structured chaos." The camp is held at a state park in a rural setting. With roughly 220 people living actively in such a close but removed environment, the group interaction is naturally chaotic at times. Some staff have sought to organize the camp in a manner in which everybody is fully aware of what is going on and why, but the Roberts have consistently avoided such initiatives.

I used to see their leadership style as a hindrance, but have come to see this "structured chaos" approach to be a significant unique aspect of camp life. The last minute planning creates a spontaneity that perpetuates a unique aspect of camp life, and perpetuates a unique excitement based on the immediacy of events and degrees of anxiety resulting from the uncertainty of what is going on and why. It should be noted essential aspects of the camp (i.e. food preparation, health care, and safety) are organized and well planned. It is the camp programming that is chaotic (by design).

The role of camp in the lives of Rush and Patsy is clearly evident. Says Patsy, "After my family, camp is the most important thing in my life." Rush is retired but had a successful career as a director of sales at a large company and he also was a motivational speaker. He attributes most of his success in business to what he's learned running the camp. They consistently praise the staff that volunteers each year.

The consciousness-raising climate of camp is nurtured throughout the week. Rush does motivational speaking, mostly with sales-related audiences, and conveys his message at camp. A consistent message is "yes you can." Campers are encouraged to take risks and try new things throughout the week. Even small achievements (i.e., eating a food item normally rejected) can be a source of humorous applause. Big achievements start with small achievements. I have, for example, taught children how to swim who never thought they could swim. The goal is to show them they'll never achieve objectives in life if they don't try. Also, there's nothing wrong with trying something new, even if you fail. There are many former campers leading successful professional lives who attribute part of their success to the encouragement they received at camp.

Camp themes typically center around what the individual can do. They are active themes. Campers are challenged throughout the week to shed assumptions of what they can and can't do. Part of this shedding process requires the dilution of peer pressures that often reinforce self-imposed limitations.

There are a variety of camp activities that indirectly and directly encourage campers to be less concerned with society norms and inhibitions. Campers and staff sing many silly/childish songs throughout the week. Often times new campers are hesitant to engage in such singing because it is childish. But when they see staff and older campers participating, most new campers will begin enthusiastic participation within a day. Campers are humorously "forced" to sing or dance at meal time. Such "performances" are wildly applauded. Thus, inhibiting society norms are dismantled and new, less restrictive norms are constructed.

This environment breeds a unique sharing and intimacy that grows throughout the week. I can offer an example from my own life. I am a "low touch" individual. That is, I do not usually touch others in the course of normal day to day interaction. However, at camp, my touching behavior increases significantly. The camp norms promote much touching in the form of hugs, embraces, and pats on the back. The increase of touching is equated with the increase of self-disclosure.

Campers, rather than staff, typically do speaking at religious services throughout the week. Speakers often share revealing thoughts they have about themselves and their lives. They receive unconditional support from the camp. This phenomena breeds more and more self-disclosure from speakers throughout the week. I define these events as a "baring of the souls." The realization that individuals can share their weaknesses, insecurities, dreams, and aspirations, and not be ridiculed, has a very positive effect. That they'll receive support from the group is almost intoxicating.

The resulting consciousness raising can, at times, serve as fertile soil for the development of new (or modified) identities. This can occur over a period of years or it can be more immediate, such as with baptism by immersion. I have never seen a dramatic disposition change but I have seen many situations where individuals have discovered a vastly enhanced self-awareness that leads to an increased self-potential. Campers who take this improved self-concept home with them have not necessarily lost their old identity, rather more often, they've added an identity to their disposition. Campers are encouraged to write a letter to themselves on the last night of camp describing their feelings about the week. The letters are collected and kept by Patsy and mailed to them at Christmas time.

The consciousness-raising experience is cultivated by a variety of factors, including the aforementioned effects of religion and utopian atmosphere. The CAMP logo, Constructing Assured and Motivated People, underscores the emphasis on consciousness raising. All aspects of camp must be interpreted with regard to this consciousness-raising phenomena.

Many of the camp activities are a means to an end, rather than an end in and of themselves. There are a variety of sports classes and outdoor activities (i.e., swimming, fishing, and hiking). The goal is not to produce greater athletes or catch big fish; rather it is to provide a climate that promotes fellowship among campers. Each cabin creates a stunt (skit) for Stunt Night. The goal is not to develop acting skills, but to promote cabin unity and stronger interpersonal relationships. Songs are sung in many of the camp settings throughout a typical camp day. The goal is not to produce excellent singing voices, but to produce a unified chorus of the collective camp mind.

The camp improves the sense of self and sense of others. The camp, since its inception, has consistently stressed interaction among diverse groups in American society. Diversity exists among campers and staff in areas such as racial and ethnic composition, economic classes, religious background, staff occupations, and residential locations (i.e., urban, suburban, and rural). Rush and Patsy actively sought to integrate the camp (racially and ethnically) in the early 1960s by establishing relations with churches with populations different than the home church. The first black person and Jewish person I met, as an example, were at camp at age ten.

There is considerable economic diversity among the campers and staff. The camp draws from the very poor and affluent of American society. Campers do not spend money at camp, they are discouraged from bringing money, so money is not an influential factor during the course of the week. The staff works to downplay economic differences among campers. Regarding religious backgrounds, camp participants have included people from a wide variety of

religious backgrounds, including atheists. Rush and Patsy consistently invite clergy from varying denominations to come to camp for the week or shorter visits as schedules permit.

Occupational diversity exists among the staff without presenting any obstacles to staff interaction and effectiveness. The staff is comprised of individuals from a wide range of occupational backgrounds (i.e., blue collar, white collar, unemployed, and so on) but manages to work well together during the camp session because the common occupation for the week is "camp counselor." Rush and Patsy consistently acknowledge God and staff as the keys to a successful camp week. Staff are frequently praised throughout each camp session.

The camp has evolved into an event for all ages, although it is specifically geared for campers in fifth through twelfth grades. As staff members marry (in some cases to other staff members) and have children, they continue to come to camp and help in ways other than as camp counselors (i.e., help in the kitchen, with classes, or special program events). Since staff children under age ten are not old enough to be part of the standard camping program, these kids frequently live with their parents in campers, empty cabins, or tents. Since most live in campers, and the campers are located in the parking lot, they are referred to as "parking lot kids" (PLKs). These younger children serve to make the camp session more of a "community," rather than a program-based, camping experience.

The camp folklore is comprised of many "folksy stories." These are stories and remembrances of camp events that Patsy will share from time to time. These evolve primarily due to the spiritual nature of the camp and the utopian atmosphere. The presence of God is frequently referenced by camp participants. The following story exemplifies such a remembrance. In 1969, Sue Lines won the theme award. The theme was "When He Calls Me" and the theme song, of the same name, stresses we should be responsive to God when he calls us. Five months after winning the award Sue died in a car accident. This event was interpreted by many as God calling Sue home to heaven. The effect of this story, and others, lead many camp participants to believe God is especially present at camp and that camp is unique because of this.

Camp is frequently described as being "special." I interpret the "specialness" as being linked to the camp environment that allows for interaction relatively free of societal inhibitions. This allows for the spiritual sense of self to evidence itself and individuals will interact with one another in a uniquely genuine manner. The collective mind of the group is strong. Patsy says she never doubts that the specialness of camp will occur. She and Rush say a quality staff ensures this environment. That is, Rush and Patsy (as camp directors) try to create an environment that allows the staff to shine and the rest comes naturally. They say the total ingredient composition of a successful camp consists of "God, staff, campers, love, program, flexibility, and food."

Camp is less a place and more a state of mind. The camp has been held at five locations since 1956 and, while the physical environment of the camp session is important, the camp locations are not necessarily considered to be "sacred ground." The sense of community, and the related interpersonal variables, are the sacred aspects of camp. Patsy points out that each time they moved the camp to a new location they feared they'd lose campers, but each time they moved, the camp population increased.

Rush and Patsy are firm believers in the American free market economic system but they make a concerted effort to diminish the role of money at camp. Campers are instructed not to bring money to camp and, even if they do bring money, there's nothing to buy. Each camper receives, as part of their camp registration fee, a camp T-shirt (with the camp theme on it), a camp photo of the entire group, and a camp yearbook. The camp yearbook lists names and addresses of all camp participants and also contains camp newspaper issues and the Morning Watch reflection sheets. Thus, interaction of participants is based more on the character of individuals rather than their material possessions.

Since the camp is independent it does not draw campers from any one particular church. Advertising is very limited. A vast majority of new campers (and staff) learn about it by word-of-mouth. News of positive experiences of participants spreads through family networks and neighborhoods. At meal times, I frequently ask campers how they heard about camp and a vast majority say from a neighbor, friend, church, or family member. I can only remember only one camper who responded, "I saw the advertisement in the local newspaper." There have been years when camp was full and kids were put on a waiting list or turned away.

When I prepared to interview Rush and Patsy I composed a list of questions covering a wide range of topics. The first question was "Are kids today different than kids thirty-five years ago?" They respond that kids today are the same as kids before them but the problems they face are different. Divorce, drugs, and alcohol are more prevalent today and are frequently variables in problems that campers encounter. Rush comments, "In 1956 our main objective was to teach swimming because many kids couldn't swim because they didn't have access to a swimming pool." Camp addresses more serious problems today. Patsy acknowledges serious problems existed then too but they tended to be kept quiet.

Rush and Patsy are adamant in their belief that kids of yesterday and today are similar in that they "want love, discipline, and direction." Once these fundamental objectives are addressed then a foundation has been laid to build in other areas.

Camp, as a subculture, provides a unique environment within which consciousness-raising communication processes allow for growth of the individual via growth of the group. Measuring the effects of this growth is very difficult because, while some changes are immediate, other changes will not occur until much later. Mental seeds can be planted at camp that don't come to fruition until long after the camper has left. Understanding the constructs of such a consciousness-raising experience is the first step toward the eventual understanding and measurement of the consciousness-raising effects. This chapter is intended as a contribution to that preliminary understanding.

References

Chesebro, J. W., Cragan, J. F., and McCullough, P. 1973. "The Small Group Technique of the Radical Revolutionary: A Synthetic Study of Consciousness Raising," *Speech Monographs* 40, 136-146.

Cragan, J. F., and Wright D. W. 1980. *Communication in Small Group Discussions*. New York: West Publishing Co.

Dickey, H. L. 1974. *The Influence of an Outdoor Survival Experience Upon the Self Concept of Adolescent Boys and Girls* (Master's Thesis, University of Montana).

Dimrock, H. S. (Ed.). 1948. *Administration of the Modern Camp*. Indianapolis, IN: Association Press.

Mitchell, A.V., and Meir, J.F. 1983. *Camp Counseling: Leadership and Programming for the Organized Camp*. Philadelphia: Saunders College Publishing.

Chapter 11

Using C-SPAN to Study Ross Perot's Expression of Sensitivity and Insensitivity with Diversity Issues during the 1992 Presidential Campaign

Communication scholars have acknowledged the use of C-SPAN as a teaching tool in resources such as *C-SPAN in the Communication Classroom: Theory and Application* (Muir 1992). This chapter describes how C-SPAN can be used for research purposes, specifically as a data base. C-SPAN research potential is exemplified through description of a study conducted to analyze the rhetoric of Ross Perot.

The primary topic of this inquiry focuses on Perot's expression of sensitivity and insensitivity with diversity issues during the 1992 presidential campaign. Perot was frequently accused of being insensitive toward diversity issues during the campaign. I analyzed the content and context of his speeches to see if there was evidence to support this claim.

C-SPAN tapes analyzed in this project were obtained from the Public Affairs Video Archives (located at Purdue University). The archives provided me with an index listing all of Perot's presentations delivered during the presidential campaign (January through November 1992) that were covered by C-SPAN. A total of fifty-five presentations are available on videotape. Fourteen of these videotapes, which are representative of Perot's presentations (in content, context, and format), were selected for analysis.

The following is a list of the selected videotapes. Videotape title, date, format, and length are listed for each presentation.

1) Life and Career of Ross Perot (March 18, 1992); American Profile Interview (1:03)
2) Perot Candidacy: American Newspaper Publishers Association; (May 5, 1992) Speech (:34)
3) University of Oklahoma Commencement Address (May 9, 1992); Speech (:21)
4) Perot Campaign Speech: NAACP Annual Convention (July 11, 1992); Speech (:35)
5) Perot Withdrawal (July 16, 1992); News Conference (:20)

6) Perot Campaign Commercial (October 6, 1992); Broadcast (:29)
7) Presidential Candidates Debate (October 11, 1992); Debate (1:36)
8) Presidential Candidates Debate (October 15, 1992); Debate (1:32)
9) Perot Campaign Commercial (October 15, 1992); Broadcast (:30)
10) Presidential Candidates Debate (October 19, 1992); Debate (1:38)
11) Perot Campaign Commercial (October 10, 1992); Speech (:31)
12) Perot Campaign Commercial (October 26, 1992); Broadcast (:31)
13) Perot Campaign Commercial (October 28, 1992); Political Event (:28)
14) Perot Campaign Commercial (October 30, 1992); Broadcast (:29)

There is no widely accepted paradigm for analyzing a speaker's sensitivity with diversity issues so this inquiry poses unique challenges. What connotates sensitivity? What connotates insensitivity? Use of C-SPAN tapes to study the aforementioned subject is particularly relevant in that the C-SPAN index helps define the sample to be studied and the tapes provide literal verbal meanings, indirect nonverbal meanings, and context for speeches. Transcripts provide literal statements but the tapes frame the literal statements. Perot was criticized after his speech to the NAACP convention, according to the Public Affairs Video Archives index abstract, for his "apparent paternalistic nature" toward minorities. Analysis of this type of criticism rests on what is said and equally on how it is said.

The hypothesis for this study is that Perot's presentations contain statements conveying insensitivity with diversity issues. The formulation of this hypothesis is based primarily on newspaper reports of Perot's aforementioned June 11, 1992 speech to the NAACP convention. *The Washington Post* reported, "Perot drew a cool reception from the group when he referred to blacks as 'you people' and 'your people'" (July 12, 1992). The *Chicago Tribune* referred to Perot's use of "you people" and "your people" as "a gaffe in his speech that offended some in the audience as racially insensitive" (July 12, 1992). This speech is significant in that the next Perot tape listed in the Public Affairs Video Archives index features Perot's withdrawal from the presidential campaign.

Data relevant to the research question of this inquiry, regarding Perot's sensitivity/insensitivity toward minority issues, were studied by viewing all the aforementioned videotapes. The data include ten hours and thirty-seven minutes of videotape. The data clearly disprove the hypothesis of this study (that Perot's presentations would contain statements conveying insensitivity with diversity issues). Perot's statements consistently convey sensitivity with diversity issues.

The following is a collection of representative statements made by Perot (regarding diversity in America). All of these statements convey sensitivity with diversity. The dates listed are referenced in the previous listing of Perot presentations analyzed in this study.

- "Our diversity is our strength, we've turned it into a weakness . . . . If you hate people I don't want your vote" (October 11, 1992).
- "If you don't mind living in a society where one out of eight women are raped I don't want your vote" (May 5, 1992).
- "We're not gonna turn the clock back. Segregating would hurt the economy" (March 18, 1992).
- "Our country will not be great until we are all united and equal . . . . I cannot be free until we are all free" (July 11, 1992).

The only speech containing comments perceived offensive is the July 11, 1992 speech to the NAACP convention. In this speech Perot's referral to the black audience as "you people" and "your people" was perceived by some to be racially insensitive. However, the NAACP is a self-defined organization (comprised of African-Americans). To refer to such a group as a distinctive entity, which the organization does with it's name and objective, does not substantiate Perot is insensitive to diversity issues. The aforementioned Perot quotes clearly establish his sensitivity with diversity.

Study of Perot is relevant in this context. He came from relative obscurity in the spring of 1992 and within seven months received 19 percent of the popular vote in the presidential campaign. He may be a powerful force in the 1996 campaign. At the 1992 "Off the (Video) Record" research conference, sponsored by the Public Affairs Video Archives at Purdue University, Perot was mentioned more than Bush or Clinton as a relevant topic for analysis in that his candidacy was so unique and without explanation.

Perot's candidacy sparked considerable debate. Scholars will no doubt be defining Perot's future in reference to his past. Findings from this type of study help set the agenda for analysis of Perot.

The research format used in this study can easily be applied with other speakers and with a variety of research questions. C-SPAN tapes allow researchers to analyze public figures in their own words, without journalistic interpretation. Public presentations can be studied in their entirety (rather than selected excerpts). Thus, C-SPAN videotapes provide an innovative database that promises to be a significant benefit to researchers of public figures and issues.

References

Muir, J. K. 1992. *C-SPAN in the Communication Classroom: Theory and Application.*
    Annandale, VA: Speech Communication Association.
"Perot addresses NAACP," *Washington Post*, 12 July 1992, 1, A10.
"Perot commits gaffe in NAACP speech," *Chicago Tribune*, 12 July 1992, p. 6.

Chapter Twelve

No Nukes: Music as a Form of Countercultural Communication

A youth culture evolved in the United States during the 1960s that, among other things, tended to reject primary norms and values of the prevailing culture in favor of a more liberal lifestyle. This culture subsequently became known as the counterculture. The counterculture has since taken a number of meanings and has been represented in various social movements.

Theodore Roszak (*The Making of A Counterculture*) and Charles Reich (*The Greening of America*) provided two primary explanations of the counterculture. Roszak discusses counterculture as arising from a youthful revulsion at technocracy. It represents a refusal to surrender spontaneity to artificiality. The counterculture serves to reassert life and joy in the face of impersonal organization (1969, chapter 2).

Reich provides a more comprehensive explanation of the counterculture that encompasses Roszak's discussion. He defines the counterculture as arising from a perception by the young of contradiction between the stated ideals of the parental generation and their actual lifestyles. He designates seven areas within this contradiction that are definitive concerns of the counterculture: (1) disorder, corruption, hypocrisy, and war; (2) poverty, distorted priorities, and law-making by private power; (3) uncontrolled technology and the destruction of environment; (4) decline of democracy and liberty, powerlessness; (5) the artificiality of work and culture; (6) absence of community; and (7) loss of self (1972, chapter 1).

Counterculture is "a term used since the mid-1960s to describe a specific form of youth culture whose members reject key norms and values of the prevailing culture" (*Encyclopedia of Sociology*, 1974, 60). Counterculture is more readily recognizable, in contrast with subculture and contraculture, through its attempts to modify, change, and alter the dominant culture.

The counterculture has influenced a variety of social movements over the years. Such movements would include, but not be limited to, the Beat Generation of the late 1950s; the antiwar, Civil Rights, Free Speech, and hippie movements of the 1960s and early 1970s; and the Women's Rights, Gay Rights, and antinuclear movements of the 1970s and early 1980s. Music festivals and concerts are a popular forum to promote the concerns of such movements and they also reaffirm the existence of the counterculture. The counterculture "constitutes a social entity which emerges en-masse at given social events such as demonstrations, rock festivals, love- ins, marches, etc., and then melts away until the next such happening" (Denisoff 1972, 156). The No Nukes concerts, held at Madison Square Garden in New York City on September 19-23, 1979, are an example of such social events.

No Nukes was presented by MUSE (Musicians United for Safe Energy). MUSE "is a group of artists and activists working for a future built on the natural power of the sun, and for an end to the threat of atomic power plants and nuclear weapons" (MUSE 1979, 2). MUSE is comprised of well known musical artists such as the Doobie Brothers; Jackson Browne; Crosby, Stills, and Nash; James Taylor; Bruce Springstein and the E Street Band; Carly Simon; Bonnie Raitt; Tom Petty and the Heartbreakers; Nicolette Larson; Poco; Chaka Khan; Jesse Colin Young; John Hall; and Gil Scott-Heron.

The No Nukes concerts were taped and MUSE subsequently released the No Nukes movie and the No Nukes album. The album is a three-record set and it contains a No Nukes pamphlet that explains the MUSE position.

> For all these reasons and more, we're devoting our own energy toward the day when not one more cent is spent on nuclear power except to decommission those plants already built and to dispose of those wastes already created. (MUSE 1979, 2)

MUSE goes on to acknowledge a countercultural context for the anti-nuclear community.

> You've already helped stop nuclear power by attending our concerts and buying this album. MUSE proceeds are being distributed to pro-solar groups around the country by the MUSE foundation, with decisions made by a board of directors designed to constitute a regional, racial, and sexual balance of activists from various segments of the anti-nuclear/pro-solar campaign. (MUSE 1979, 2)

The statement regarding racial and sexual equality evidences the interdependence of countercultural concerns.

The purpose of this chapter is to examine the music of the No Nukes concert as a form of countercultural communication. This examination will be prefaced with a discussion of the theoretical parameters that establish music as a form of communication.

Irvine and Kirkpatrick performed an experimental study that found the following assumptions in support of music being viewed as a standard form of communication:

> First, the musical artist is engaged in a rhetorical activity to the extent to which he manipulates a symbol system (sound, rhythm, words, and tempo) to react to and modify the dominant philosophical, political, religious, and aesthetic values of both general and specific audiences. Second, the musical form changes a message from its normal discursive state into a form that possesses more aesthetic and kinesthetic appeal. Third, the normal listening situation gives the musical artist greater freedom of expression than would normally be employed by the speaker. (Irvine and Kirkpatrick 1972, 272)

Knupp documented the tendency of protest songs to use various rhetorical shortcuts that are not consistent with deliberative public discourse. "They (protest songs) are allowed this luxury, I take it, because they are a form of in-group rhetoric. The predispositions of the group promote the acceptability of symbolic shorthand" (Knupp 1981).

Similarly, Roth found song lyrics to communicate characterization and ideas in "Folk Song Lyrics as Communication in John Ford's Films." "In particular, the song lyrics express thematic reverberations—the affirmation of community and nature—that are integral to Ford's work (Roth 1981).

Music has been recognized as a form of communication from a variety of contemporary perspectives (Kosokoff and Carmichael 1970). Music has also been recognized as a form of communication from more historical perspectives. Gleason quotes Plato as warning:

> Forms and rhythms in music are never changed without producing changes in the most important political forms and ways . . . the new style quietly insinuates itself into manners and customs and from there it issues a greater force . . . goes on to attack laws and constitutions, displaying the utmost impudence, until it ends by overthrowing everything, both in public and private. (Gleason 1971, 94)

Reich provides similar emphasis on the importance of music in his description of the counterculture. He does this because the counterculture is expressed through a variety of cultural channels and the impact of the meanings collectively expressed through these channels create the total effect. Reich classifies the counterculture ("new generation") as Consciousness III.

> When we turn to the music of Consciousness III, we come to the chief medium of expression . . . . Music has become the deepest means of communication and expression for an entire culture. (Reich 1974, 260)
> The music has achieved a relevance, an ability to penetrate to the essence of

what is wrong with society, a power to speak to man "in his condition" that is perhaps the deepest source of its power. (Reich 1974, 268)

Roszak also stresses the pertinence of music as expression within the counterculture: "Much of what is most valuable in the counterculture does not find its way into literate expression. . . . Timothy Leary is probably correct in identifying the pop and rock groups as the real 'prophets' of the rising generation" (Roszak, 1969, 291). Roszak recognizes both the lyrics and style of countercultural music. He acknowledges "one probably hears the most vivid and timely expression of young dissent not only in the lyrics of the songs but in the whole raucous style of their sound and performance" (Roszak 1969, 291).

The importance of music as countercultural communication is a widely accepted position. This should be no surprise given the consistent popularity of music in the U.S. youth culture. In the period under study, music with countercultural themes was popular in the youth culture. "The hub of the counterculture, given its experiential nature, is the musical genre of rock, from where come the heroes or 'high priests' of counterculture, the rock musicians" (Denisoff 1972, 157).

> In this sense, sixties rock became a musical indicator of the concerns, anxieties, and motives of at least a portion of a generation attempting to establish a standpoint from which to comprehend and react to these events. But at most it summoned from youth a token form of participation in the counterculture. (Robinson, Pilskaln, and Hirsch 1976)

"In the minds of young people, five hundred pages of realistic experience in David Copperfield appears to have less impact on their lives than a two to five minute rock song which reflects experiences just as realistic, but in more contemporary language" (Nyquist 1972). "The poetry of politics is rock music. Once we begin to think of it this way, the power and direction of the music begin to make sense" (Gleason 1971, 146).

As mentioned earlier, the purpose of this chapter is to examine the music of the No Nukes concert as a form of countercultural communication. There are twenty-eight songs on the three-album set. Eight of these twenty-eight songs emphasize countercultural concerns and three of the eight songs deal specifically with the antinuclear movement. To analyze these eight songs for their countercultural significance, the song lyrics will be compared against Reich's seven primary concerns of the counterculture, which were previously outlined in this chapter (Reich 1972, 4-8). These seven primary concerns serve as definitive parameters of the counterculture.

The eight songs that will be analyzed are "Power," "Plutonium Is Forever," "We Almost Lost Detroit," "The Times They Are A-Changin'," "Long Time Gone," "Takin' It To The Streets," "Teach Your Children," and "Get Together." Analysis will be limited to the lyrics of the songs. All seven of Reich's primary concerns of the counterculture are evidenced in the eight songs.

The three anti-nuclear songs ("Power," "Plutonium Is Forever," and "We Almost Lost Detroit") contain the most pointed lyrics, regarding countercultural concerns. Of these, "Power" received the most acclaim and radio play. "Power" is recognized as the theme song of the No Nukes movement and it addresses several of Reich's countercultural parameters.

In "Power" the lyrics stress the importance of the antinuclear position because live are at stake, both in the present and in the future. The future is stressed because much of what we are doing now in the nuclear industry will affect future inhabitants of the earth. Given the gravity of the issue the artists emphasize that since the nuclear issue affects us all, everybody needs to make a conscience decision to oppose nuclear power. The song then yearns for a simpler and safer approach by using the sun as a source of solar energy. This relates well to a general countercultural theme of simplicity and peaceful connectivity with the environment. The appeal of returning biogradable wastes to the soil is also stressed. The chorus closes by pleading that the nuclear waste is a form of atomic poison and that we must rid ourselves of this poison if we are to survive.

The concern most evident in "Power" and the other two antinuclear songs, as stated by Reich, is "3) uncontrolled technology and the destruction of environment" (Reich 1972, 5). The last line of the song clearly indicates the position of the song. The middle of the chorus emphasizes a move back to the basics of life, which involves concerns "6) absence of community" and "7) loss of self" (Reich 1972, 7).

"Plutonium Is Forever" carries a reggae beat and is described, on the album, as a Caribbean no nukes song. The opening part of the song emphasizes strong implications with countercultural concern "3) uncontrolled technology and the destruction of environment" (Reich 1972, 5).

In this opening the lyrics posit the idea that perhaps mankind is cursed. This curse is evidenced by the self-destructive and polluting habits linked to our excessive lifestyles in the United States. The song alludes to the damage we are doing to the sky and the ocean. The artists go on to predict that if the counterproductive behavior continues it will lead to the end of our society as we know it. The song also hints at concern "2) poverty, distorted priorities, and law-making by private power" (Reich 1972, 5).

"We Almost Lost Detroit" deals with a partial meltdown that occurred at a nuclear power plant in Detroit, Michigan. "Beginning on October 6, 1966, plant operators confronted a partial meltdown that could have led to an explosion and the release of a huge cloud of radioactive poisons into the Motor City" (MUSE 1979, 6). This song is a clear indictment against nuclear power. Countercultural concern "3) uncontrolled technology and the destruction of environment" is evident (Reich 1972, 5).

"We Almost Lost Detroit" approaches the antinuclear position abstractly. It paints a picture of a nuclear power plant that exists in a world of its own out on a distant highway and describes it as being from a different reality. It is recognized as promoting curiosity from children. Children are used symbolically to represent innocent inquiry and also as the ones who stand to lose their future through no doing of their own. They are portrayed as victims. The song then goes on to acknowledge that they are describing a Detroit nuclear power plant and how that power plant almost blew up and, if it had, it would've wiped out Detroit. It then describes this situation as a madness and one that must be avoided.

"We Almost Lost Detroit" goes on to acknowledge the controversial death of Karen Silkwood, a former employee of a plutonium factory in Oklahoma, who was killed when her car was allegedly forced off the road and into a concrete abutment. She was on her way to meet with a *New York Times* reporter to reveal evidence of unsafe and illegal practices at the plutonium factory. Her research folder, which was in the car at the time, was never found (MUSE 1979, 9).

The song speculates about what Karen Silkwood would say to us if she were still alive. This conveys the image that we should be inspired by her sacrifice and intentions to reveal the problems of the nuclear power industry. The lyrics go on to cynically describe how the financial forces of the nuclear power industry win over the safety of the people and how such a scenario explains how Detroit could have been lost in a nuclear accident that does not need to happen. As before, this situation is associated with madness.

In early 1979, a U.S. District Court judge tried the case and the Silkwood family was eventually awarded $500,000 for Karen's suffering and the plutonium factory was fined $10 million "for 'wanton and reckless' disregard for the safety of its workers" (MUSE 1979, 9). The song's discussion of the Silkwood case stresses the symptoms of countercultural concern "2) poverty, distorted priorities, and law-making by private power" (Reich 1972, 5).

"We Almost Lost Detroit" underscores five of the seven concerns outlined by Reich. In addition to concerns 3 and 2, the song highlights concerns "1) disorder, corruption, hypocrisy, and war"; "4) decline of democracy and liberty, powerlessness"; and "7) loss of self" (Reich 1972, 4-7).

The remaining five songs to be analyzed earned their popularity during the late 1960s and early 1970s. These songs do not emphasize antinuclear issues, but they do address paralleled countercultural concerns.

"The Times They Are A-Changin'" was written by Bob Dylan in the mid-1960s and has since been recorded by various artists. The song, like the other songs that do not emphasize antinuclear issues, is more abstract in its statement of countercultural concerns and it serves as an overall warning.

In the song, Dylan broadcasts an appeal to all people from the various areas of society. He instructs that we should look beyond many of the rationalizations we live with and acknowledge that there are serious signs of trouble that we should be aware and worried about. The song goes on to speculate conditions will no doubt get worse before they get better because these signs of trouble will become more severe and eventually engulf us. He illustrates this by comparing it to being surrounded by flood waters and how, if we want to survive, we'll need to swim against the currents of change.

This song stresses elements of concerns "(1) disorder, corruption, hypocrisy, and war"; "(5) the artificiality of work and culture"; and "(7) loss of self" (Reich 1972, 4-7). Dylan wrote numerous songs that the counterculture embraced but "The Times They Are A-Changin'" was one of his most popular songs.

"Long Time Gone" is another song which was written in the late 1960s. It paints a bleak picture about the the state of society and points to the need for listeners to speak out against the chaos that exists. The primary weapon for combating social ills, according to the song, is to be honest and speak your mind. However, it is acknowledged that speaking the truth can put the speaker at risk. The song takes a shot at politicians by suggesting we not seek political office because, if we do, it is a sign that we have sold out on our values. This is symbolically addressed when the lyrics say if you go into politics you will need to cut your hair. Cutting your hair is correlated with shedding your values. The song closes by warning it will be a long time before we experience the dawn of truth.

"Long Time Gone" focuses on concerns "(1) disorder, corruption, hypocrisy, and war" (Reich 1972, 4) and "(4) decline of democracy and liberty, powerlessness" (Reich 1972, 6). Much like "The Times They are A-Changin'," "Long Time Gone" provides an overall warning from the counterculture.

Takin' It To The Streets" is sung from a different perspective. It is particularly unusual because it gives a statement from the oppressed. It acknowledges at the outset that we are all connected even though we may think of ourselves as living in different social classes. The oppressed singer explains he lives in what most listeners would think of as a living hell and that the middle-class could not begin to understand the plight of his community.

This introduces a resounding complaint from the perspective of the oppressed that is a dominant theme in the song.

The singer complains that the middle and upper-class continually say that they are going to help the lower echelons of society who are at risk but this help never materializes in a meaningful way. A vague threat is issued that if conditions do not improve, the impoverished members of society will take matters to the streets as a means of making their plight known.

As a statement from the oppressed, this song bases its threat from countercultural concern "(2) poverty, distorted priorities, and law-making by private power" (Reich 1972, 5). Also evidenced are concerns "(6) absence of community"; "(1) disorder, corruption, hypocrisy, and war"; "(7) loss of self"; and "(4) decline of democracy and liberty, powerlessness" (Reich 1972, 6-7).

"Teach Your Children" and "Get Together" are pleas for the future. "Teach Your Children" makes distinctions between the older and younger generations. Compared to most of the other songs in this collection it is more compassionate and optimistic. The song was written during a period when there was a considerable generation gap between the youth culture and their parents. The song stresses that the youth culture should not easily dismiss the perspectives maintained by their parents, which are based on life experiences and very real to the individual. It promotes the idea that each generation can help the other. The youth culture can offer optimism and the parent generation can share its experience.

The song explains that the older generation has been a victim of concerns "(1) disorder, corruption, hypocrisy, and war"; "(2) poverty, distorted priorities, and law-making by private power"; and "(7) loss of self" (Reich 1972, 4-7). It suggests the younger generation can help the older generation overcome concerns "(6) absence of community" and "(7) loss of self" (Reich 1972, 7).

"Get Together" makes a similar suggestion without emphasizing the generational differences. It emphasizes that we are all empowered to make choices in life that can lead to good or bad results, but that we should instinctively be oriented toward the choices that will have positive results. Fears and anxieties about the present and future are recognized as being understandable and expected. The key to unlocking the bonds of such anxieties and fears is to look for the good in our fellow human beings. The song stresses we can do this in very simple ways on a day-to-day basis and from this perspective we can build toward a better tomorrow one day at a time, each of us in our own way.

"Get Together" is an optimistic song in that it stresses the simplicity with which we can live together in harmony. The key is in our outlook on life and how we convey that outlook with each other. This song attributes most problems to concern "(1) disorder, corruption, hypocrisy and war (Reich 1972,

4). It explains that to deal with these problems we must first work on concern "(6) absence of community" (Reich 1972, 7)

These eight songs were written from different perspectives and various social problems are highlighted. All seven of Reich's primary concerns of the counterculture are addressed within the songs.

MUSE is comprised of eighteen musical acts. Eight of these acts sang the songs selected for analysis in this article: "Power" (Doobie Brothers, John Hall, and James Taylor), "Plutonium Is Forever" (John Hall), "We Almost Lost Detroit" (Gil Scott-Heron), "The Times They Are A-Changin'" (James Taylor, Carly Simon, and Graham Nash), "Long Time Gone" (Crosby, Stills, and Nash), "Takin' It to the Streets" (Doobie Brothers and James Taylor), "Teach Your Children" (Crosby, Stills, and Nash), and "Get Together" (Jessie Colin Young).

Denisoff states there are two categories of songs of persuasion. The magnetic song "appeals to the listener and attracts him to a specific movement or ideology within the ranks of adherents by creating solidarity in terms of the goals expressed in the propaganda song." The rhetorical song is "designed to point to some social condition, describe the condition, but offers no ideological or organizational solution such as affiliating with a social movement; the rhetorical song poses a question or a dissent" (Denisoff 1972, 60-61). The songs analyzed in this chapter are rhetorical songs of persuasion. They point to social conditions but they offer vague direction for the listener to take in dealing with the social conditions described.

The purpose of this chapter was to examine the music of the No Nukes concert as a form of countercultural communication. After establishing music as a form of communication and acknowledging the importance of music within the counterculture, eight songs were selected from the concert album due to their countercultural emphasis and the lyrics of these songs were compared against Reich's seven primary concerns of the counterculture. Analysis of the songs found that all seven of Reich's primary concerns of the counterculture are addressed in the lyrics.

Scholarly treatments of popular music generally use one of two methodological techniques: opinion survey and content analysis of song lyrics. I have utilized content analysis in this article. As a closing comment, I am compelled to acknowledge the importance of the music itself, as opposed to the lyrics or the opinions held about the music. "The music itself is rarely treated despite the acknowledgment by several students of the important role of tonal and aesthetic structures of popular songs" (Denisoff and Levine 1971). "I recognize that one probably hears the most vivid and timely expression of young dissent not only in the lyrics of the songs but in the whole raucous style of their sound and performance" (Roszak 1969, 291).

Gonzalez and Makay emphasize rhetorical ascription in "Rhetorical Ascription and the Gospel According to Dylan." "Using chord progressions and instrumentation designed to represent moods, feelings, and meanings to accommodate lyrical purpose, Dylan's gospel seeks high ascriptive value with listeners" (Gonzalez and McKay 1983, 14).

The intensity of merely reading the lyrics of "Power" is magnified by hearing "Power" played on a stereo. The intensity of "Power" is magnified considerably when the listener is swaying to the music with thousands of other people when the song is performed at a No Nukes rally. The intensity of a song can vary, depending on the experiential context experienced by the listener.

References

Bloodworth, J.D. 1975. "Communication in the Youth Counterculture: Music as Expression," *Central States Speech Journal* 26, 304-309.

Crosby, D. 1979. "Long Time Gone," *No Nukes: From the MUSE Concerts for a Non-Nuclear Future* (Record Album). Jackson Browne, Graham Nash, John Hall, and Bonnie Raitt (Producers). Los Angeles: Asylum Records.

Denisoff, R.S. 1972. *Sing a Song of Social Significance.* Bowling Green, OH: Bowling Green University Press.

Denisoff, R.S., and Levine, M.H. 1971. "The One Dimensional Approach to Popular Music: A Research Note," *Journal of Popular Culture* 6, 911.

Dylan, B. 1979. "The Times They Are A-Changin'," *No Nukes: From the MUSE Concerts for a Non-Nuclear Future* (Record Album). Jackson Browne, Graham Nash, John Hall, and Bonnie Raitt (Producers). Los Angeles: Asylum Records.

Encyclopedia of Sociology. 1974. Guilford, CT: Dushkin Publishing Group.

Gonzalez, A., and Makay, J.J. 1983. "Rhetorical Ascription and the Gospel According to Dylan," *Quarterly Journal of Speech* 69, 1-14.

Gleason, R.J. 1971. "A Cultural Revolution," in R.S. Denisoff and R.A. Peterson, eds., *The Sounds of Social Change.* Chicago: Rand McNally.

Hall, J., and Hall, J. 1979. "Plutonium is Forever," *No Nukes: From the MUSE Concerts for a Non-Nuclear Future* (Record Album). Jackson Browne, Graham Nash, John Hall, and Bonnie Raitt (Producers). Los Angeles: Asylum Records.

———. 1979. "Power," *No Nukes: From the MUSE Concerts for a Non-Nuclear Future (Record Album).* Jackson Browne, Graham Nash, John Hall, and Bonnie Raitt (Producers). Los Angeles: Asylum Records.

Irvine, J.R., and Kirkpatrick, W.G. 1972. "The Musical Form in Rhetorical Exchange: Theoretical Considerations," *Quarterly Journal of Speech* 58, 272- 273.

Knupp, R.E. 1981. "A Time for Every Purpose Under Heaven: Rhetorical Dimensions of Protest Music," *The Southern Speech Communication Journal* 46, 388.

Kosokoff, S., and Carmichael, C.W. 1970. "The Rhetoric of Protest: Song, Speech, and Attitude Change," *The Southern Speech Communication Journal* 35, 302.

McDonald, M. 1979. "Takin' It to the Streets," *No Nukes: From the MUSE Concerts for a Non-Nuclear Future* (Record Album). Jackson Browne, Graham Nash, John Hall, and Bonnie Raitt (Producers). Los Angeles: Asylum Records.

MUSE (Musicians United for Safe Energy). 1979. *The MUSE Record Book.* New York: MUSE.

Nash, G. 1979. "Teach Your Children," *No Nukes: From the MUSE Concerts for a Non-Nuclear Future* (Record Album). Jackson Browne, Graham Nash, John Hall, and Bonnie Raitt (Producers). Los Angeles: Asylum Records.

Nyquist, E.B. 1972. "Music as Communication," *Vital Speeches* 38, 202.

Powers, C. 1979. "Get Together," *No Nukes: From the MUSE Concerts for a Non-Nuclear Future* (Record Album). Jackson Browne, Graham Nash, John Hall, and Bonnie Raitt (Producers). Los Angeles: Asylum Records.

Reich, C. 1972. *The Greening of America.* New York: Random House.

Robinson, J.P., Pilskaln, R., and Hirsch, P. 1976. "Protest, Rock and Drugs," *Journal of Communication* 26, 135.

Roszak, T. 1969. *The Making of a Counterculture.* Garden City, NY: Anchor Books.

Roth, L. 1981. "Folk Song Lyrics as Communication in John Ford's Films," *The Southern Speech Communication Journal* 46, 396.

Scott-Heron, G. 1979. "We Almost Lost Detroit," *No Nukes: From the MUSE Concerts for a Non-Nuclear Future* (Record Album). Jackson Browne, Graham Nash, John Hall, and Bonnie Raitt (Producers). Los Angeles: Asylum Records.

Thomas, C.I. 1974. "'Look What They've Done to My Song Ma': The Persuasiveness of Song," *The Southern Speech Communication Journal* 39, 260-268.

Chapter Thirteen

Communication Strategies for Reducing Patient Anxiety in Pedodontic Dentistry

This chapter will discuss the use of selected communication behaviors for reducing the level of anxiety experienced by child dental patients. The main areas to be covered are communication within dentistry, communication with children in the dental environment, and approaches for reducing anxiety experienced by child dental patients.

Dentists comprise the second largest group of primary, direct-service health practitioners in the country (Young and Smith 1972). Little has been written on communication between dental professionals and their patients, in comparison with other primary health care areas. Dental communication is unique, in comparison with other health care areas, as there is a lack of urgency in everyday interactions. Dental care is rarely a matter of life and death (Thompson 1986, 88).

A problem more prevalent in dentistry than in most of medicine is pain, or more specifically, the fear of pain. This reaction to dental work is partially one of fear of the unknown, which may include pain. This problem is complicated as many people don't go to see a dentist unless they have a problem, which is much more likely to result in pain when treated. Thus, a self-fulfilling prophecy can occur (Thompson 1986, 90). One study of dental patients indicates pain, and the equipment usually associated with pain, accounts for 62 percent of patient fears (Arnold 1985).

Communicating with children in health care settings, specifically the dental environment, poses a variety of considerations for the dental team. These considerations include the health care environment, the child's age, interpersonal relationships, and helping children understand their dental experience.

Mark Knapp has researched the strong effect physical context has on human communication. The physical setting can exert a powerful influence on interaction by affecting expectations of patients and providers and inhibiting their exchanges (Knapp 1978). Dental offices can be frightening to children.

They are comprised of unfamiliar people, strange instruments and equipment, unpleasant sounds, and are often decorated in a manner that creates a stark, sterile, and cold atmosphere.

Obviously, all stressful aspects of the dental office cannot be eliminated but some helpful approaches can serve to dilute fears. Unfamiliar people can be identified by title and name. Equipment can be decorated with mobiles and artwork, or they can be placed out of sight until they are needed. Cheerful pastel colors can be used to replace antiseptic white on walls. Children's art work can be displayed on walls for viewing from the dental chair, and toys and books can be placed in waiting areas (Klinzing 1985).

The age of the child is also a consideration. Children ages one to five years frequently exhibit the most difficulty with health care experiences. Researchers attribute this to three primary reasons: (1) the child is separated from the parents (Robertson 1962); (2) young children have a more pronounced sensitivity to pain and an inability to deal with fears (Levy 1945); and (3) young children do not have strong reality concepts and therefore are subject to grotesque fantasies (Chapman, Loeb, and Gibbons, 1956). The dental team can help compensate for these vulnerable areas by making special efforts to provide young children with additional emotional support.

The dental team cannot be expected to replace the support group of a child, but researchers have found the establishment of positive interpersonal relationships between health professionals and pediatric patients can help reduce the threat experienced by children (Dimock 1962). Such relationships can be initiated by talking with children about general topics of interest such as movies, sports, pets, and hobbies. Patient perception of caring feelings conveyed by health care providers is essential in attending to the emotional needs of patients. Through communication, caring feelings are translated into caring behavior. Research indicates practitioners' displays of caring and warmth can increase patient satisfaction (Doyle and Ware 1977) and increase patient compliance with treatment (Caplan and Sussman 1966).

A considerable amount of research indicates child understanding of health care experiences reduces emotional upset (Wolfer and Visintainer 1975). Possibilities for misinterpretations are fostered when the child does not understand procedures he or she is being subjected to. Researchers have found children frequently interpret illness as punishment for wrong doing (Gellert 1958) and health care procedures can be interpreted as hostile, mutilating acts (Erickson 1958). It has been shown that a practitioner's explanations of procedures improves patient compliance (Lane 1982). Thus, the dental team would be well advised to explain, in understandable terms, a basic description of what the child will be experiencing.

When appropriate, the use of humor can be used to alleviate anxieties. A study titled "Joking Under the Drill" indicates the use of humor may reduce the subjective experience of stress (Trice 1986). Trice found those patients who exhibited joking-laughter behaviors rated their dental experiences as being less stressful.

The dental team should be aware of the content and relationship conveyed in communication. That is, when a dentist interacts with a patient, messages occur on two levels: content and relationship. Thus, a verbal message not only provides information, it also defines the relationship of the interactants. This relationship is defined through elements such as tone of voice, body movements, eye behavior, and other nonverbal areas (Wilmot 1979).

Nonverbal communication is widely accepted as being more influential than verbal communication. When nonverbal messages contradict verbal messages, the nonverbal messages will be believed over verbal messages (Knapp 1978). It is imperative for dental team members to be aware child dental patients interpret both verbal and nonverbal messages. These nonverbal messages are sent through a variety of behaviors, including artifacts, kinesics, occulesics, tactilics, proxemics, and chronemics.

Artifacts refer to our personal appearance. Such considerations include clothing, jewelry, and hair style. In the past decade, the traditional white uniforms female dental team members generally wore have been substituted by some with less formal types of clothing. Regardless, clothing sends a message (good or bad) that affects patient observations.

Kinesics deals with body movements and posture, which can convey listener interest, involvement, and alertness. In working with children, it is important to request changes in body movements and posture in a way that ensures their understanding of why they are being asked to change positions—for instance, being leaned back in a dental chair or being sat up to rinse the mouth.

Occulesics involves facial and eye movements. The face and eyes are primary sources of emotional information for patients. Dental team members should be aware of facial and eye movements they are presenting as patients often watch the face of who is working on them. If the dental team member occulesically communicates fear, anger, or disgust, the patient will most likely interpret this. Friendly facial and eye expressions help to accommodate the patient, just as friendly conversation does.

Tactilics refers to touching behaviors and is one of the more intimate channels of human communication. Dental team members can communicate empathy with their touch or they can communicate aversion through insensitive touching behavior. Touching behavior is especially important when the patient is having his or her teeth worked on. Practitioners suggest a variety of methods for alleviating child patient fears of injections, drilling, and polishing. For example, one approach before cleaning teeth is to polish a fingernail of the patient to show what the instrument will feel like. Injections can be given less painfully by rubbing the gum prior to and during the injection. Children may also want to hold (or squeeze) the hand of a dental team member. In each situation, touching behaviors can benefit the patient.

Chronemics deals with the use of time. Dental team members should be sensitive to the amount of time patients spend in waiting rooms, dental chairs, and being worked on while in the dental chair. Making a child patient wait for dental treatment can increase that patient's anxiety level. Empathy with the patient can be an appropriate guide for chronemic concerns.

Proxemics involves the use of space and distancing. Practitioners have to infringe on cultural territoriality norms when working on patients. This closeness can cause patient discomfort. When possible, the dental team member should give the patient time and space between phases of dental treatment to allow him or her to feel spatial privacy.

It is important for dental team members to remember the aforementioned factors, verbal and nonverbal, are perceived in concert, rather than individually. Practitioners should strive to be aware of the messages they are sending and ensure these messages do not contradict each other. In situations where the patient is unaware of dental procedures, as is frequently the case with children, dental team members can make the difference between a positive or negative experience.

References

Arnold, W. E. 1985. "Communication Patterns of Dentists with Their Patients." Unpublished paper.

Caplan, E., and Sussman, M. 1966. "Rank Order of Important Variables for Patient and Staff Satisfaction," *Journal of Health and Human Behavior* 7, 133-138.

Chapman, A., Loeb, D., and Gibbons, M. 1956. "Psychiatric Aspects of Hospitalizing Children." *Archives of Pediatrics* 73, 77-78.

Dimock, H. G. 1960. *The Child in the Hospital.* Philadelphia: Davis.

Doyle, B. J., and Ware, J. E., 1977. "Physician Conduct and Other Factors that Affect Consumer Satisfaction with Medical Care," *Journal of Medical Education* 23, 283-292.

Erickson, F. 1958. "Play Interviews for Four-Year-Old Hospitalized Children." *Monographs of the Society for Research in Child Development* 12, 3.

Gellert, E. 1958. "Reducing the Emotional Stresses of Hospitalization for Children," *American Journal of Occupational Therapy* 12, 125-129.

Gordon, G. E., Dugan, J. E., Wilcox, E. M., and Wilcox, J. R.. 1986. "Communicating with Patients: Messages from Nursing Uniforms," Paper presented at the Communicating with Patients Conference, Tampa, Florida

Klinzing, D. and Klinzing, D. 1985. *Communication for Allied Health Professionals.* Dubuque, IA: William C. Brown.

Knapp, M. L. 1978. *Nonverbal Communication in Human Interaction.* New York: Holt, Rinehart and Winston.

Lane, S. D. 1982. "Communication and Patient Compliance," in L. S. Pettegrew, P. Arntson, D. Bush, and K. Zoppi, eds., *Straight Talk: Explorations in Provider and Patient Interaction.* Louisville, KY: Humana.

Levy, D. M. 1945. "Child Patients May Suffer Psychic Trauma after Surgery," *Modern Hospital* 65, 51-52.

Robertson, J. 1962. *Hospitals and Children.* London: Victor Gollancz.

Thompson, T. L. 1986. *Communication for Health Professionals.* New York: Harper and Row.

Trice, A. D. 1986. "Joking Under the Drill: A Validity Study of the Coping Humor Scale," *Journal of Social Behavior and Personality* 2, 265-266.

Wilmot, W. W. 1979. *Dyadic Communication.* Reading, MA: Addison-Wesley.

Wolfer, J. A., and Visintainer, M. A. 1975. "Pediatric Surgical Patients' and Parents' Stress Responses and Adjustment as a Function of Psychological Preparation and Stress Point Nursing Care," *Nursing Research* 24, 244-255.

Young, W. O. and Smith, L. 1972. "The Nature and Organization of Dental Practice," in H. Freeman, ed., *Handbook of Medical Sociology.* Englewood Cliffs, NJ: Prentice-Hall.

Chapter Fourteen

The Hospital Chaplain and the Perpetuation of Understanding in the Health Care Environment

Understanding in the health care environment is created and affected by a number of variables. The hospital chaplain is one such variable and he or she is the focus of this chapter. The hospital chaplain works with other members of the health care team to promote understanding, but does so more by helping the patient to interpret his or her situation rather than understanding his or her specific illness. The hospital, as a health care organization, can be studied as a representative organizational structure. The concept of organizational culture is a viable perspective from which organizations can be studied (Deal and Kennedy 1982).

Such study is grounded in an appreciation of the organizational culture phenomenon. Definitions and applications are provided by a variety of theorists such as Harris (1985, 5) and Pacanowsky and O'Donnel-Trujillo (1982, 122). Organizational culture is defined as "the unique sense of the place that organizations generate through ways of doing and ways of communicating about the organization. Organizational culture reflects the shared realities in the organization and how these realities create and shape organizational events" (Shockley-Zalabak 1988, 65). The culture of an organization is comprised of elements such as shared norms, rites, rituals, and stories that provide the members with a unique symbolic common ground (Pacanowsky and Putnam 1983, 100). All organizations, including health care institutions, have such cultures.

The perception process is significantly affected by the physical context within which the perceptions occur (Arnold 1989). The health care facility influences interactions among the health care consumer and health care providers by affecting their expectations and inhibiting their exchanges. When patients enter huge structures, such as medical centers, the intimidation process can begin before they even meet a health care professional. This situation can be perpetuated by the internal environment that frequently includes mazelike hallways, desks used as barriers, paging systems, medical equipment, and an extensive use of antiseptic white. The intimidation can become more complex when health professionals become so familiar with the physical setting that they do not notice its effect on their interaction with patients (Klinzing and Klinzing 1985, 26). Similar effects of the physical environment on human interaction have been noted by Baum and Valins (1973, 211-212).

Organizational structure is an element of the physical context. The organizational structure of health care institutions is usually hierarchical. Authority and responsibility rest at the top and descend through subordinate levels. Also, specific functions are maintained by components in the structure, such as departments and positions, while formal communication networks unite the various elements (Klinzing and Klinzing 1985, 177). These organizational perspectives help to describe the organizational culture of each health care institution. Other unique characteristics affect communication within health organizations. These include urgency of activities, status differences, educational differences, and gender socialization differences (Thompson 1986, 14-15). Each patient must learn to adapt to the particular health care institution culture and understand his or her role within the unique functioning of the organization.

"A primary objective of health education programs is to increase the individual's acceptance and responsibility for his/her own state of health" (Hicks, Spurgeon, and Stubbington 1988, 15). "Certain general positions have emerged in the literature regarding the contributory role of psychosocial factors to . . . rehabilitation" (Colonese, Fontana, Kerns, and Rosenberg 1989, 175-176). Although research indicates the need for patient orientation programs (Sharf and Poirier 1988, 225), usually there is little formal orientation for the patient. It is surprising health care practice has not been affected by health care research regarding implementation of formal orientation programs or some type of patient education.

The orientation of patients to the health care environment is most beneficial when it is provided as the patient first enters the health care setting. At this point the patient has fewer misconceptions regarding what will happen during his or her stay. The concern with timing is an important communication variable in health education. Ideally, a formal orientation session to instruct and clarify misunderstandings would be helpful. In practice, this function is usually informally handled by various members of the health care team, including the hospital chaplain. Patient orientation, be it positive or negative, occurs the same way first impressions are created in interpersonal communication. If information is not provided to inform the patient, he or she will seek answers to questions to better understand his or her health care experience. The answers he or she finds may or may not be accurate.

It will be helpful to clarify the existence of health care teams and the function of the chaplain as a member of the health care team. Health care teams have evolved during the past forty years. Three factors led to theory development: (1) medicine has become more specialized and there is a need for specialists to work collectively as a team; (2) the technology of medicine has become much more complicated and there is a need to integrate the talents of varied specialists to use this complicated technology; and (3) an increasing concern with the whole patient (including the spiritual life of the patient). That is, medical problems cannot be understood without looking at the patient as a person (Thompson 1986, 24).

In *Psychology of Pastoral Care*, Paul Johnson addresses the third factor in a fairly subjective manner.

> The wise physician knows that health is an inner harmony of many vitalities not to be attained by materia medica alone, but rather by restoring the whole personality to well-functioning relationships. . . . As a member of the health care team, the chaplain offers his spiritual ministrations. . . . The chaplain specifically has a psychological role to perform; he works not with medical tools but with spiritual instruments that operate in the cure of souls. (1952, 204-205)

This view, although written in the 1950s, is equally relevant today.

The objective of the hospital chaplain is to work with the mind and soul rather than with curing physical problems. James P. Arnold, director of pastoral care at All Children's Hospital in St. Petersburg, Florida, relates, "The chaplain is not there to remove suffering so much as to help people find its deeper meaning for their lives. This is done, in part, by reassuring the sufferer that the struggle is worth it, that meaning is ultimately to be found because God has deemed the sufferer to be meaningful" (Arnold 1986, 2). With such an objective, the communicative role of the chaplain is not only emphasized, it is essential. His or her communicative abilities are a big part of the foundation for his or her effectiveness.

The pastoral counseling literature clearly stresses the communicative role of the hospital chaplain. Howard Clinebell, in *Basic Types of Pastoral Care and Counseling*, describes a variety of models, approaches, and concerns within pastoral counseling (1984, 94-209). The expression of caring feelings is of primary importance throughout the pastoral counseling processes. "Caring feelings are essential in providing for the emotional needs of patients. Through communication, caring feelings are translated into caring behavior" (Klinzing and Klinzing 1985, 7). Aday and Anderson (1975) have conducted empirical research showing that displays of caring and warmth by health care team members can increase patient satisfaction. However, the desire to help can lead to burnout if the health care professional becomes consistently over involved (Miller, Stiff, and Ellis 1988). Realizing this is the first step toward combating the problem.

Herman K. Knodt, director of pastoral care at Grant Hospital, in Columbus, Ohio, emphasizes the chaplain should speak the "patient's language." It is important for expressions of caring to be offered in language that is understood by the patient. That is, the chaplain needs to gauge the level of understanding that the patient is capable of and converse with the patient in a manner easily understood by the patient. One idea can be expressed at a variety of language levels (Knodt 1986). The chaplain needs to consistently consider if his or her language level is appropriate for the receiver.

The chaplain's communicative role involves a ministry of dialogue. This makes language usage especially relevant. If the receiver is not familiar with the terminology used by the sender he or she has little to rely on, regarding the interpretation of meaning, except contextual cues. The accuracy of these contextual cues may or may not be reliable. Thus, chaplain sensitivity with patient language norms is pivotal to his or her success in providing counsel.

The stress on language is a building block for the emphasis on dialogue. "It is a ministry of conversation, of the mutual exchange of ideas and feelings, both verbally and nonverbally. . . . All professions in the hospital engage in dialogue with patients. But it is done in concert with other services and activities. Dialogue is the primary service and activity of chaplains. If not done with sensitivity and skill, it leaves the chaplain with little else to offer" (Arnold 1986, 1). It is an essential tool for the chaplain.

The effective chaplain will consistently seek ways to develop communicative skills that enhance the work of the health care team. These skills can serve to enhance the patient orientation process. The communicative role of the chaplain within the patient orientation process draws considerably on chaplain listening skills. Listening skills are a primary factor in enabling the chaplain to empathize with the patient's situation (Becker 1985, 33). Unfortunately, listening is a communication behavior that seems to be taken for granted (Spearritt 1962). As a listener, it is important for the chaplain to respond to feelings expressed, rather than to the intellectual content of patient messages. This can be difficult, as ministerial training emphasizes the intellectualization of beliefs and the importance of finding the "truth" in terms of intellectually formulated propositions (Wise 1951, 71). Thus, the chaplain must be aware of dynamics that can enhance his or her understanding of the patient's perceptions and work to benefit the patient with this awareness.

The chaplain listens to patient views about the hospital environment and policies as he or she helps the patient become oriented. Based on what is understood, he or she can be instrumental in minimizing patient anxiety by providing additional information and guidance regarding what will happen during the patient's visit. For instance, "They'll get you up at 7:30 A.M., you will take a shower, they will give you an injection, and about a half hour later roll you down a long hallway. I will be with you when they take you from your room" (Knodt 1986).

There can easily be situations where the patient does not fully understand medical procedures. In such situations the chaplain can request the appropriate health care team member to clarify the area(s) in question for the patient. The assertion that the offering of information improves patient compliance has been confirmed by Francis, Korsch, and Morris (1969). It is in such instances that the hospital chaplain can use his or her rapport with other members of the health care team to benefit the patient. Some health care providers may be requested to provide instruction more than once and may resent such requests of their time. The chaplain can diplomatically put the need in perspective for health care team members.

In another area, empirical studies indicate the expression of caring feelings also improves patient compliance with treatment. This finding was substantiated by Becker, Drachman, and Kirscht (1972). Thus, the chaplain would be well advised to communicate enough information to meet patient needs, and to do so in a caring manner. The same would hold true for other health care team members as well. "Only since the late 1960s, with the growth of new medical schools and the initiation of post-graduate residencies emphasizing primary care, did instruction in communication—typically offered under such labels as 'clinical interviewing', 'interpersonal skills,' 'introduction to clinical medicine,' or even 'behavioral science'—formally become part of medical education" (Sharf and Poirier 1988, 225). The continued emphasis on such areas evidences the relevance of these topics.

The primary purpose of this chapter has been to acknowledge the role of the hospital chaplain in the perpetuation of understanding in health care settings. The information presented has underscored the complementary communicative role played by the hospital chaplain in helping the health care team engage in effective communication practices. It should be clear that explicit guidelines for achieving effective communication practices cannot be concretely established because situational variables vary so much. It is another function of the hospital chaplain to be sensitive to such situational variables and consider them as he or she works with the patient and health care team.

Analysis of understanding in health care environments, and obstacles to it, reveal those factors that compose the organization. When the influence of these factors is understood, awareness of such effects can enhance patient orientation into the health care institution setting. The roles of health care team members, including the hospital chaplain, are highlighted in this process and this high lighting can be the foundation for improved understanding among health care team members and with their patients.

References

Aday, L.A., and Anderson R.A. 1975. *Access to Medical Care*. Ann Arbor, MI: Health Administration Press.

Arnold, E., 1989. *Interpersonal Relationships: Professional Communication Skills for Nurses*. Philadelphia, PA: W.B Saunders Co.

Arnold, J.P. 1986. "Patient, Family, Staff Communication: A Chaplain's Perspective." Paper presented at the "Communicating with Patients" conference, University of South Florida.

Baum, A. and Valins, S. 1973. "Residential Environments, Group Size, and Crowding," *Proceedings of the American Psychological Association*.

Becker, A.H. 1985. *The Compassionate Visitor*. Minneapolis, MN: Augsburg Publishing.

Becker, M.H., Drachman, R.H., and Kirscht J.P. 1972. "Motivations as Predictors of Health Behavior," *Health Services Reports* 87, 852-861.

Clinebell, H. 1984. *Basic Types of Pastoral Care and Counseling*. Nashville, TN: Abingdon Press.

Colonese, K.L., Fontana, A.F., Kerns, R.D., and Rosenberg, R.L. 1989. "Support, Stress, and Recovery from Coronary Heart Disease: A Longitudinal Causal Model," *Health Psychology* 8.

Deal, T.E., and Kennedy A.A. 1982. *Corporate Cultures: The Rites and Rituals of Corporate Life*. Reading, MA: Addison-Wesley.

Francis, V., Korsch, B.M., and Morris, M.J. 1969. "Gaps in Doctor-Patient Communication," *New England Journal of Medicine* 280, 535-540.

Harris, T. 1985. "Characteristics of Organizational Cultures: A Communication Perspective," paper presented at the annual meeting of the Speech Communication Association, Denver, Colorado.

Hicks, C., Spurgeon, P., and Stubbington, J. 1988. "The Importance of Psycho-Social Variables in Changing Attitudes and Behavior," *Health Education Journal* 47.

Johnson, P.E. 1952. *Psychology of Pastoral Care*. Nashville, TN: Abingden Press.

Klinzing, D., and Klinzing, D. 1985. *Communication for Allied Health Professionals*. Dubuque, IA: Wm. C. Brown.

Knodt, H.K. Personal interview, May 9, 1986.

Kreps, G. 1988. "Communication and Health Education in Health Care Delivery," paper presented at the annual meeting of the Speech Communication Association in New Orleans, Louisiana.

Miller, K.I., Stiff, J.B., and Ellis, B.H. 1988. "Communication and Empathy as Precursors to Burnout Among Human Service Workers," *Communication Monographs* 55.

Pacanowsky, M. and Putnam, L.L. 1983. *Communication and Organizations: An Interpretive Approach.* Beverly Hills, CA: Sage Publications.

Pacanowsky, M. and O'Donnel-Trujillo, N. 1982. "Communication and Organizational Cultures," *Western Journal of Speech Communication* 46.

Sharf, B.F. and Poirier, S. 1988. "Exploring (Un)Common Ground: Communication and Literature in a Health Care Setting," *Communication Education* 37.

Shockley-Zalabak, P. 1988. *Fundamentals of Organizational Communication.* New York: Longman Press.

Spearritt, D. 1962. *Listening Comprehension—A Factual Analysis.* Melbourne, Australia: G.W. Sons.

Thompson, T.L. 1986. *Communication for Health Professionals.* New York: Harper and Row.

Wise, C.A. 1951. *Pastoral Care: Its Theory and Practice.* New York: Harper and Brothers.

Part Three

Qualitative Interpretations in Education, Classroom and Research

Chapter Fifteen

The Use of Self-Help Subliminal Tapes as an Experiential Learning Tool

This chapter describes a study that was conducted to investigate the validity of a claim that audio cassette tapes containing subliminal messages can improve public speaking ability. The study is relevant for instructors of public speaking in that, if the claim is legitimate, such tapes could supplement standard instruction in public speaking classrooms. If the claim is not legitimate then the study is useful in that such tapes will be exposed as being fraudulent.

I first learned of the subliminal tapes described in this study when I read an advertisement for them in the *Chronicle of Higher Education*. I see the *Chronicle of Higher Education* as a reputable source of information dealing with higher education issues. An organization called Midwest Research of Michigan had placed an advertisement promoting the subliminal audiotapes.

Background of the Study

Claims for subliminal programs that improve one's ability to speak in public are viewed with skepticism. Advertisements in the popular media make such claims that seem to be nothing more than unethical approaches to swindling people out of their money. How can listening to a tape with no discernable human sound, with only the sound of ocean waves, improve public speaking ability?

Many Americans have been exposed to claims about the dramatic benefits of listening to subliminal self-help tapes through magazines, newspapers, and television. Martin Block and Bruce Vanden Bergh (1985) conducted a telephone survey of 330 adults to determine consumer attitudes toward the use of subliminal stimulation techniques in a self-improvement product. The study found consumers to be skeptical toward the use of subliminal messages for self-improvement and concerned about being influenced to do something they did not want to do. Those consumers most favorable toward the subliminal technique had prior experience with computers and video equipment and appeared to be less educated, younger, and more often married than those subjects less favorable toward the subliminal technique.

Judging from the increase in advertisements for subliminal programs, it is obvious many people believe these programs work. It is important for behavioral scientists and professors of public speaking to conduct independent investigations on the effect of subliminal messages on public speaking ability.

This chapter will describe a study that examines the effect of subliminal messages on public speaking ability. Speculation on the effect of subliminal messages is common in the popular literature (Key 1980) but little has been done to prove such speculation in grounded terms. Advertisements claim subliminal messages can improve our lives in many ways. The purpose of this study is to examine such a claim in a concrete manner that provides more substantiation than mere speculation.

Midwest Research of Michigan, under the SCWL trademark (Subconscious to Conscious Way of Learning), produces seventy-one audio-cassette programs that claim to help users improve their lives by helping them lose weight, stop smoking, control stress, improve sexual satisfaction, overcome fears, control drinking, improve study habits, improve in golf, and improve in many other areas. Program 57, *Effective Speaking*, claims to help the user gain poise and confidence in public speaking.

Need for the Study

If the academic community can disprove the claimed effects of these types of subliminal programs, then we will do the public a service by sharing our research. If our research substantiates these claims, then we can also share our findings. If the latter is true, perhaps we can then investigate how such subliminal programming works and use it to benefit our teaching. Although these claims are unwarranted, it is not fair to dismiss claims of subliminal success simply because it is a new and unsubstantiated approach. Otherwise, the world might still be considered flat. The purpose of this study is to investigate the effectiveness of subliminal techniques for improving public speaking ability.

The Hypothesis

The research hypothesis of the experiment states: College students who listen to selected subliminal messages will not develop more observed skill in public speaking than college students who listen to tapes containing no subliminal messages. The operational or test hypothesis states: Students who use subliminal tape programs designed to improve public speaking ability will perform no differently than classmates who listen to identical sounding placebo tape programs containing no subliminal messages. The independent variable is use of the SCWL subliminal program 57, *Effective Speaking*. The dependent variable is the observed and perceived skill in public speaking. Final semester grades in a college-level Public Speaking course will be accepted as evidence for this study.

Definition of Terms

Control Group: Those subjects who unknowingly use a placebo tape that sounds identical to the subliminal tape but contains no subliminal messages.

Experimental Group: Those subjects who use a subliminal tape.

Placebo: A harmless neutral pill, treatment, or process that has the look and feel of the actual drug or treatment for which it has been secretly substituted.

Subliminal: Any sound, smell, touch, taste, or visualization that exists but is below the level of conscious perception.

Assumptions

The study is based on the following assumptions. The research techniques of this study are valid measures of the variables in the study. Subjects' questionnaire responses are accurate and honest measures of these variables. The cooperative (student-involved) grading process is an accurate and valid measure of public speaking ability.

Limitations

The sample size was small because participation was limited to volunteer students enrolled in two sections of a public speaking course, in attendance on the day the experiment started, and who continued in the class until the end of the term. Some of the students who participated were absent from class on the day pretest questionnaires were administered and were excluded from the study. The sample is not a true random sample. Assignment to experimental and control groups was done by a double blind process of random assignment.

Scope

The study focuses on the use of subliminal learning as a synergistic instructional technique to work in concert with conventional instructional methods and not as a stand-alone process. Subjects are from a single major midwestern urban university and all have the same public speaking professor.

Review of Related Research

Adams (1957) summarized the findings of seventy-six studies of behavior without awareness. He concluded that subjects have been able to discriminate among many types of auditory and visual stimuli presented below the threshold of awareness to a degree greater than chance.

Review of literature dealing with the success of subliminal messages in *modifying behavior* shows a lack of substantiated research in this area. There are a variety of works that speculate on the effects of subliminal messages (Adams 1982; Key 1973; Key 1980; Morse and Stoller 1982; Packard 1981) but few of these substantiate their claims. The following review provides a description of some of the more grounded works.

Laboratory research established that humans can perceive auditory, visual, and olfactory stimuli that are below the level of conscious awareness (DeFleur and Petranoff 1959). Messages flashed on a movie screen every five seconds for about 1/1000 of a second, during a film, have proven to affect audience behavior (Morse and Stoller 1982). It is important to acknowledge that this technique will not influence anyone who is not already predisposed to the specific suggestion given (Morgan, Morgan, and Kole 1985). Thus, an individual could not be influenced to murder a random victim unless already predisposed to such an idea.

George Smith, author of *Motivation Research in Advertising and Marketing*, affirms, "There is evidence that people can be affected by subthreshold stimulation; for example, a person can be conditioned to odors and sounds that are just outside the range of conscious awareness" (Packard 1957, 133). Corrigan and Becker (1956) found information can be subliminally communicated to the unconscious and then used later by the recipient at the conscious level.

Silverman (1983) describes an experimental design using symbiotic fantasies for alleviating anxiety. His procedure involved the use of a tachistoscope, a projector that quickly flashes visual stimuli, to subliminally project words such as "Mommy and I are one." In 1986, the U.S. government included the same technique in a stress management seminar for federal executives. The subliminal messages included "I am calm," "I deserve to feel safe," and "Mommy and I are one." The last message, according to the seminar psychologist, "gives people a feeling of safety and security" (*People Magazine* 1986).

Silverman has conducted or directed roughly sixty studies showing that subliminal presentation of emotionally charged messages can initiate unconscious thoughts and feelings and eventually alter behavior. Furthermore, he has derived that wish-related subliminal stimuli and the power to activate psychodynamic processes can affect overt behavior.

Audio subliminal messages are claimed to be effective in many areas. Borgeat, Chabot, and Chaloult (1981) reported positive results in their study of smokers, alcoholics, and obese patients who were subliminally influenced to reduce cigarette, alcohol, and food intake.

Hollingworth (1985) describes two studies that used subliminal messages to reduce theft. The studies highlight the significant reduction of theft in an Australian supermarket and stores in the United States (Becker, Chamberlain, Heisse, and Marino 1982).

Using a tachistoscope, Kenneth Parker (1982) showed that subliminal messages were effective in improving academic performance. Sixty students enrolled in a summer law course were divided into three groups of twenty. The two experimental groups earned higher grades than the control group.

In a similar study, Harold Cook (1985) examined the effect of a subliminally presented symbiotic gratification, and magic of believing message, on academic achievement of fifty-four graduate students. Subjects were randomly assigned to either an experimental message group or a control message group and received on the average of twelve sessions, ten exposures per session, of four-msec visual subliminal presentations of one of the three messages. Experimental group messages were either "Mommy and I are one," or "I understand statistics (or measurement)." The control group message was "People are walking." Each session occurred just before the lecture, in either a statistics or a measurement class. Each course was taught by regular faculty who were unaware of the experimental conditions. Objective final examinations for each course revealed statistically significant differences in favor of the symbiotic gratification experimental condition over the control condition. Differences between the two experimental groups were not significant.

Auditory subliminal learning

The present study is concerned with a more practical application of subliminal communication for improving academic performance, specifically in the public speaking course. Several tests using subliminal sound are relevant to this study.

Swanson (1985) used Potentials Unlimited subliminal tapes with nursing students preparing for a state licensing examination. The subjects were instructed to listen to the tapes everyday for the forty-eight days before the test. Members of the control group listening to ocean wave tapes scored 2060 on their test. Members of the experimental group listening to ocean waves containing subliminal messages scored 2183, more than 120 points higher, on the state board examination.

Morgan, Morgan, and Kole (1985) used subliminal techniques for improving academic performance. College students who unknowingly used SCWL programs designed to increase recall in test situations outperformed their classmates who listened to identical sounding placebo tapes containing no subliminal messages. This double blind study yielded two important results. First, the subliminal group reported an increase in the number of hours spent in study and the control group reported a decrease. By the end of the experiment, the subliminal group reported spending sixteen hours per week in study and the control group had reduced their study time to eleven hours. The most important difference was in academic performance. The subliminal group quality point grade average went from 2.28 to 2.73, while the control group average dropped .01 from 2.47 to 2.46. In other words, the subliminal group went from "C" up to "B-" while the control group average of the students who listened to ocean waves without subliminal messages did not improve.

This study focuses on a practical application of subliminal communication for improving academic performance, specifically in the public speaking course.

Methods and Procedures

The purpose of this study was to test the effectiveness of subliminal suggestions for improvement of public speaking skills. The methods used in this study will be described in the following order: variables selected and sample population.

Variables selected for study

This study has attempted to determine the effect of exposure to subliminal suggestions on improvement in public speaking skills. The independent variable (input) for this study is SCWL subliminal program 57, *Effective Speaking*, produced by Midwest Research of Michigan. The dependent variable is the final course grade in public speaking for each participating student. Other variables considered were age, sex, years of college, credit hour load, grade point average, course grade expectations, self-appraisal of speaking skills, self-confidence, self-report of enjoyment of public speaking, hours of speech preparation, frequency of tape use, evaluation of tape sound, and type of tape player used.

Midwest Research offered use of subliminal tapes to qualified researchers through announcements in several editions of the *Chronicle of Higher Education* (1986). The company accepted the proposal and agreed to provide subliminal and control tapes for the study. They reported that their subliminal scripts deal with self-image, attitude, and confidence in addition to the topic of the particular program. SCWL program 57, *Effective Speaking*, was chosen for study. Midwest Research supplied forty tapes of program 57 free of charge. Half the tapes contained the subliminal program and the other half were placebo tapes (with no subliminal messages). From a table of random numbers, the assistant director of research at Midwest Research labeled the twenty experimental tapes.

Then the missing numbers in the forty number sequence were used to label the control tapes. It was by chance that the twenty-six volunteers in attendance at the time the experiment started drew an equal number of experimental and control tapes. Following completion of data collection and after final course marks were reported, Midwest Research provided a list of tape numbers showing which tapes were subliminal and which were placebo.

Sample population

The test covered a ten-week period from early January to mid-March, during the winter quarter at the University of Cincinnati. Students in two sections of the public speaking course were invited to participate in the study. A total of twenty-six students successfully completed the project. Most of the participants were in the 18-28 age group and in their freshmen and sophomore years. The entire sample consisted of thirteen males and thirteen females, with a "B-" group average, and enrolled in fifteen credit hours.

Of the twenty-six tapes issued to those volunteering, thirteen were subliminal tapes (experimental group) and thirteen were placebo tapes (control group). To the conscious ear, all the tapes were recordings of ocean waves, gulls, and crickets. Instructions to participants included the following:

1) Participation is not required. You will not be penalized for nonparticipation or rewarded for participation.
2) A company that produces self-improvement tapes has provided these tapes for study free of charge. The company claims using these tapes can improve your public speaking ability. I am testing their claim.
3) You will receive a tape if you choose to participate. Play it as often as you like (preferably three to seven times a week). Mark the cassette case each time you listen to it. I will collect the tapes at the end of the term.
4) Do not listen to the tape while driving or working with machinery. You can play the tape while working around the house, cooking, cleaning, studying, watching television, eating, or similar activities.

Measurement

The subjects completed a pretest questionnaire that was administered by the professor at the time the tapes were distributed. The posttest questionnaire was completed ten weeks later when the tapes were returned. On the day the tapes were issued, each student signed a Research Enrollment Acknowledgment that further described the purpose of the information collected. Subjects completed questionnaires the day the tapes were collected.

A *double blind* condition existed because neither the students nor the professor who administered the collection of data knew which tapes were experimental and which were control. Double blind random assignment was accomplished by the way that the tapes were issued. Each tape had a code number on it. Students wrote their code number on their pretest questionnaires. After final grades were recorded at the end of the term, Midwest Research sent the list of numbers to identify subliminal and placebo tapes.

Experimental Design

Group	Pretest	Treatment	Post-test
Experimental	Survey	Home use of subliminal program for ten weeks	Survey and final course grade
Control	Survey	Home use of a placebo program for ten weeks	Survey and final course grade

Analysis of Data

Data used in this analysis consists of the pretest survey, posttest survey, and the final grade in the public speaking course. The double blind code was broken after course marks were turned in to discover which students had actual subliminal tapes (experimental group) and which ones had the placebo (control group). Table 15.1 shows that most of the participants were in the 18-28 age group and in their freshmen and sophomore years. The entire sample consisted of thirteen males and thirteen females.

Table 15.1 Age Distribution of Subjects

Age	Experimental	Control	Total
18-28	10	12	22
29-38	2	1	3
39 up	1	0	1
Total	**13**	**13**	**26**

Table 15.2 Speech Grade, Prior Grade Point Average, and Academic Load

	Experimental	*Control*
Grade for public speaking course (4.0 scale)	2.23	1.80
Prior grade point average (4.0 scale)	2.80	2.73
Time preparation each speech	140 min.	180 min.
Weekly listening to tape sound	90 min.	90 min.
Average course load	15.45 credits	15.15 credits

Table 15.3 Expected Grade in Public Speaking

Expected	Experimental		Control	
Mark	*Pre – Post*		*Pre - Post*	
A	1	2	4	0
B	12	9	8	12
C	0	2	1	2

Table 15.2 lists final grade averages for experimental and control groups, average minutes the tape was played each week, and the average number of hours spent preparing for each speech. The subliminal group received a higher final course grade average (2.23) than the placebo group (1.80). The averages are on a 4.0 scale. Members of both groups indicated they listened to their tapes an average of three times a week. Each side of the tape plays for thirty minutes. The subliminal group members averaged two hours twenty minutes preparing for each speech and the placebo group averaged three hours preparing for each speech. Both groups were similar in credit hours attempted during the quarter tested. Grade point averages for the two groups were similar at the start of the study. Both groups averaged just over fifteen credit hours attempted with previous grade point averages of 2.8 for the experimental (subliminal group) and 2.73 for the control (placebo group).

Table 15.3 shows student expectations of their course grades. Expectations within both groups centered in the "B" range. Grade expectation averages dropped slightly, within the "B" range, between the pretest and posttest surveys.

Table 15.4 shows the group averages of the self-evaluation ratings at the beginning and end of the course. Both groups expected similar improvement in their abilities to speak comfortably before an audience. Both groups expressed similar improvement in their perceptions of how well they were understood by audience members. Both groups reported similar improvement in confidence when speaking in front of an audience.

Self-evaluation of public-speaking ability improved for both groups, with the placebo group evaluating themselves higher in this area. In comparison with friends, both groups thought that their speaking ability improved, with the placebo group reporting the most gain. Student pretest perceptions of possible enjoyment of public speaking class experiences were the same in both groups. However, the placebo group showed a higher level of enjoyment on the posttest.

Table 15.5 notes the types of tape players used by the students and their general reaction to the tapes. More students used stereo systems than portable tape players. Most of the participants found the tapes to be pleasant and relaxing. About one-third of the students thought the tapes were either peculiar or unpleasant.

Table 15.4 Self-Evaluation of Public Speaking Ability (on a 4.0 scale)

Item	Experimental	Control
	Pre – Post	*Pre – Post*
1. Comfortable speaking to group	2.69 - 3.92	2.85 - 3.92
2. Easily understood	2.92 - 3.69	3.31 - 3.85
3. Confident speaking to group	2.85 - 3.69	2.62 - 3.69
4. Effective public speaker	2.62 - 3.23	2.85 - 3.85
5. Better public speaker	2.69 - 3.15	2.69 - 3.92
6. Enjoy speaking in class	4.07 - 4.15	4.08 - 4.54

Table 15.5 Tape Player and Sound Quality (number of students)

Type	Experimental	Control	Total
Portable	4	6	10
Stereo	8	7	15
Unknown	1	0	1
Peculiar/unpleasant sounds	4	5	9

Summary

The purpose of this study was to investigate the effectiveness of a subliminal technique for improving public speaking ability. In this double blind study the sample consisted of twenty-six volunteer subjects. I did not know which tapes were experimental or control until after the data was collected.

The operational hypothesis states: Students who use subliminal tape programs designed to improve public speaking ability will perform no differently than classmates who listen to identical sounding placebo tape programs containing no subliminal messages. Based on the data collected, the hypothesis of no difference is rejected. The average final course grade in public speaking for subliminal tape users was .43 higher than for the placebo tape users. On a 4.0 scale, the subliminal users marks averaged 2.23 and placebo users marks averaged 1.80. While this is not a radical difference, it does warrant attention. The final grades were determined before the double blind code was broken. The students and I did not know which students were in the experimental and control groups until after final grades were computed and reported to the office of the registrar.

Self-evaluations between subliminal and placebo groups did not differ much although minor differences did occur. The variations were in areas of public speaking ability compared with friends, enjoyment of the course experiences, and speech preparation time. Placebo users evaluated themselves higher than the experimental group in effectiveness, public speaking ability compared with friends, and enjoyment of the course experiences. Subliminal tape users averaged spending two hours and twenty minutes preparation time per speech, while placebo users averaged three hours. Oddly, the subliminal tape users achieved an average final course grade .43 higher (on a 4.0 scale) than the placebo group.

Thus, placebo users evaluated their abilities higher, worked longer hours in preparation, and did worse on the final course grade average than the subliminal tape users. This replicates the findings reported by Morgan, Morgan, and Kole (1985) where the subliminal tape users rated themselves lower than their counterparts who used placebo tapes, but who improved .45 over prior cumulative averages, while placebo group grade average did not improve.

Need for further study

Based on the findings of this study, the differences in final course grade averages substantiates the need for more research on the use of subliminal programs for educational applications. Research is needed in three areas: first, replication of the experimental design used in this study to investigate a possible consistency of findings; second, study of the importance of how often the tape should be used for optimal results (Students in this study listened to their tapes an average of three times a week. If they listened to them twice as much would the programming be twice as effective?); third, study of how this type of subliminal programming might be effective.

The use of subliminal programming poses interesting possibilities in a variety of areas besides public speaking. More research is needed to verify the claims made by organizations that produce such subliminal programming. This study serves as groundwork for such verification efforts.

References

Adams, J.K. 1957. "Laboratory Studies of Behavior Without Awareness," *Psychological Bulletin* 54 , 383-405.

Adams, V. 1982. " Mommy and I Are One," *Psychology Today* 16(5), 24-36.

Becker, H.D., Chamberlain, S.B., Heisse, J.W., and Marino D.R. "Subliminal Communication and Hypnosis," paper presented at the Conference of the American Society of Clinical Hypnosis, in Denver, Colorado.

Block, M.P., and Vanden Bergh, B.G. 1985. "Can You Sell Subliminal Messages to Consumers?" *Journal of Advertising* 14(3), 59-62.

Borgeat, F., Chabot, R., and Chaloult, L. 1981. "Subliminal Perception and Level of Activation," *Canadian Journal of Psychiatry* 26(4), 255-259.

Borgeat, F., Elie, R., Chaloult, L., and Chabot R. 1985. "Psychophysiological Responses to Masked Auditory Stimuli," *Canadian Journal of Psychiatry* 30(1), 22-27.

Chronicle of Higher Education. 1986, June-August issues.

Cook, H. 1985. "Effects of Subliminal Symbiotic Gratification and the Magic of Believing on Achievement," *Psychoanalytic Psychology* 2(4), 365-371.

Corrigan, R.E., and Becker, H.C. 1956. *Research Report*. Rome, NY: Rome Air Development Command.

DeFleur, M.L., and Petranoff, R.M. 1959. "Television Test of Subliminal Persuasion," *Public Opinion Quarterly* 23(2), 168.

Hollingworth, M. "Subliminal Tapes Halve Thefts in Chain Store," *Retail World* 30 January, 1985, 14.

Key, W.B. 1973. *Subliminal Seduction*. Englewood Cliffs, NJ: Prentice-Hall.

———. 1980. *Clam Plate Orgy*. Englewood Cliffs, NJ: Prentice-Hall.

Morgan, D.L., Morgan, P.K., and Kole, J. *Effect of Subliminal Messages on Academic Performance* (Report No. 2). Clarion, PA: Center for Independent Research.

Morse, R.C. and Stoller, D. 1982. "The Hidden Message that Breaks Habits," *Science Digest* 90, 28.

"Our Tax Dollars at Work," *People Magazine*, December 1986, 14.

Packard, V. 1957. *The Hidden Persuaders*. New York: David McKay.

Packard, V. 1981. "The New (and Still Hidden) Persuaders," *Reader's Digest* 118(4), 120.

Parker, K.A. 1982. "Effects of Subliminal Symbiotic Stimulation on Academic Performance: Further Evidence on the Adaptation-Enhancing Effects of Oneness Fantasies," *Journal of Counseling Psychology* 29(1), 19-28.

Silverman, L.H. 1976. "The Reports of My Death Are Greatly Exaggerated," *American Psychologist* 31, 621-637.

Silverman, L.H. 1983. *The Search for Oneness*. Bloomington: Indiana University Press.

Swanson, H.J. 1985. "The Improvement of Test Performance through the Use of a Subliminal Hypnosis Tape," Ph.D. dissertation, Nova University, Florida.

Chapter Sixteen

Experiential Learning of Nonverbal Communication in Popular Magazine Advertising

Nonverbal communication is recognized as a primary influence in the human interaction process. This chapter focuses on nonverbal communication in popular advertising and how such advertising exemplifies various areas within nonverbal communication theory.

To work toward these ends I not only seek to show students examples of nonverbal communication in popular advertising, I also try to involve them in the research process, thus allowing them to work with me in selecting examples of popular advertising that evidence nonverbal communication areas. We used popular magazine advertising, in this particular project, as a data base for this experiential learning process.

Experiential learning offers the student an opportunity to learn by doing through hands-on application. It is learning "in which the learner is directly in touch with the realities being studied" (Keeton and Tate 1978, 2). This process involves "not merely observing the phenomenon being studied but also doing something with it, such as testing the dynamics of the reality to learn more about it, or applying the theory learned about it to achieve some desired results" (Keeton and Tate, 2). This type of learning can be achieved in or outside the traditional classroom environment.

David Kolb has developed the idea of experiential learning into a theory of the learning cycle. Kolb believes "experience is translated into concepts which in turn are used as guides in the choice of new experiences" (Kolb 1976, 2). He describes the learning cycle as consisting of four interdependent steps: (1) immediate concrete experience is the basis for, (2) observation and reflection, (3) which is assimilated into the formation of abstract concepts and generalizations from which implications for action are deduced, and (4) followed by testing implications of concepts in new situations. Kolb states step four leads to step one (concrete experience) and thus the cycle is complete (Kolb 1976, 2-3). Experiential learning is unique in comparison with mere lecture as it uses a variety of our senses not often used in lecture environments. I developed this project to provide students an opportunity to build from information provided in class lectures with the objective of helping them learn by being able to understand and apply fundamental nonverbal communication concepts.

The project lasted seven weeks (of a ten-week quarter) and included participation from two sections of the basic interpersonal communication course at the University of Cincinnati. It involved ten primary steps.

1) The class was divided into groups to review a wide variety of popular magazines (i.e., *Newsweek, Cosmopolitan, Rolling Stone, Reader's Digest,* and so on).
2) They collected advertisements that exemplified nonverbal communication areas discussed in class lectures and assigned readings.
3) We complied collected advertisements under various nonverbal communication classification areas (i.e., kinesics, proxemics, objectics, and so on). An advertisement was placed in a classification area when the behavior in the photograph exemplified a nonverbal communication behavior. For example, an advertisement with two people looking into each other's eyes exemplified eye behavior. Student groups submitted advertisements in various nonverbal categories and defended their submissions with the instructor.
4) We looked through the advertisements in each nonverbal communication classification area to see which classification areas were best exemplified by the advertisements collected. Primary criteria for this process was the quality of the photographs (regarding their depiction of the nonverbal areas). Quantity of advertisements was a secondary criteria. We narrowed the nonverbal communication classifications to six areas, from a field of twelve, which we focused on in the presentation. The six areas were physical characteristics, artifacts, kinesics, touching behavior, proxemics, and environmental factors.
5) Ten advertisements were chosen for photographing in each of the six nonverbal classification areas. Criteria for selection were based on the degree to which the photograph depicted the particular nonverbal behavior. The photographed advertisements were developed into slides.
6) The slides were organized into the aforementioned six nonverbal areas.
7) We wrote a script describing the six nonverbal categories and how these categories were observed in popular magazine advertising. Description of popular magazine advertising was based on the advertisements chosen for inclusion in the six nonverbal areas.
8) Background music was selected for portions of the presentation. Criteria for selection were based on our ability to adapt musical lyrics to meanings portrayed in the six nonverbal areas.

9) An audiocassette tape was recorded (narration and music). The tape included an introduction, description of the six nonverbal areas, discussion of selected advertisements that depict each of the six nonverbal areas, emphasis on the relevance of these depictions, and a conclusion. Slides wereorganized in an order that supported and complemented the audio tape.

10) The final product was presented in class.

This project was completed during the winter term of 1987, and was intended to serve as a experiential learning tool for the two sections participating in the production. A second objective was to produce a presentation that could be used to describe nonverbal communication concepts during future instruction in sections of the basic interpersonal communication course at the University of Cincinnati.

After completion and observation of the presentation, each student who participated in the production of the presentation was asked to write a brief one-page report on his or her involvement in the project as a learning experience. I asked each to respond to the following questions:

A) Was this project a positive learning experience? If yes, why? If no, why not?

B) How did your participation in this type of project affect your learning of nonverbal communication areas (as opposed to using lecture as a means of learning the material)?

C) The nonverbal communication areas covered in the project will be included on the final examination. Has your participation in the project enhanced your learning of these concepts enough to ensure correct answers to exam questions?

Thirty four students participated in the production of the presentation and thirty-three of them completed the evaluation assignment. Student responses to these questions indicated their participation in the project was enjoyable and a positive learning experience. The following numerical categories correspond with the aforementioned question areas.

A) All students completing the evaluation assignment indicated it was a positive learning experience. Responses generally indicated their participation was positive because they learned the material and enjoyed being actively involved with the learning process.

B) A vast majority of the thirty-three students completing the evaluation assignment indicated their initial understanding of the nonverbal communication areas was based on class lectures and assigned textbook readings.

However, they emphasized the project gave them an opportunity to build from this information considerably and better understand its applications and relevance in their day-to-day interactions. The ability to apply the information and understand its relevance seemed to be the primary benefit of participation in the project.

C) The final examination had six questions dealing with the six nonverbal communication areas covered in the project. All the students felt participation in the project enhanced their understanding of the six nonverbal areas. Thirty-three of the thiryt-four students taking the final examination answered all six nonverbal communication questions correctly while one student missed two of the six questions.

Students in both sections completed a written survey that quizzed them on their knowledge of the six main categories of nonverbal communication covered in the presentation, and solicited their views on the effectiveness of the presentation in helping them better understand nonverbal communication. A copy of this survey is included in Survey 16.1.

Thirty-eight students (from both sections) observed the presentation and completed the survey. Thirty-five of these students answered all six matching questions correctly, which involved matching the nonverbal category with the correct definition. The remaining three students answered four of the six matching questions correctly.

Participants were asked to respond to the following statement: "The presentation has helped me better understand nonverbal communication and how it exists within society." Thirty-seven percent "strongly agreed," 55 percent "agreed," and 8 percent were "neutral." No participants "disagreed" or "strongly disagreed" with the statement.

The use of this project as an experiential learning tool was beneficial to the students who worked on the project and the product of the experiential efforts has also served well as a teaching aid for other sections of the basic interpersonal communication course. The aforementioned discussion of responses from students who worked on the project clearly indicates they perceived their learning experience to be enhanced due to their participation in the learning process. Their abilities on the final examination support this contention.

Students who observed the presentation exhibited a correct understanding of the nonverbal concepts (as found in the survey) and indicated agreement that the presentation benefited their learning of the material. Comparison of the students who produced the presentation versus the students who only observed the presentation indicates that while both groups learned the material, the students who produced the presentation gained a more thorough appreciation of the application and relevance of the nonverbal communication concepts. This can be attributed to the degree they worked with the nonverbal materials and their active participation in the learning process.

Students who produced the presentation experienced an enhanced learning opportunity. According to Keeton and Tate, this enhanced learning experience occurred because the students did not merely observe the phenomena being studied, but they also applied the theory to achieve a desired result (Keeton and Tate 1978, 3). Active participation in the learning process provided the bridge to this enhanced learning experience.

The students who produced the presentation experienced Kolb's learning cycle described earlier in this paper. *Concrete experience* was used as a basis for *observation and reflection,* which was assimilated into the *formation of abstract concepts and generalizations* which led to *testing implications of concepts in new situations* (Kolb 1976, 2-3). As described by Kolb, these four steps lead to the initial step of concrete experience.

References

Keeton, T. and Tate, J. 1978. *Learning By Experience—What, Why, How.* San Francisco: Jossey-Bass Inc..

Kolb, D. A. 1976. *Learning Style Inventory: Technical Manual.* Boston: McBer and Co.

Survey 16.1

_____ Physical characteristics   A. deals with clothing, jewelry,
                                            and beauty aids

_____ Artifacts   B. deals with body shape, hair
                                            color, and similar traits

_____ Kinesics   C. deals with the expression of
                                            emotions such as loving,
                                            caring, etc.

_____ Touching behavior   D. deals with body movements
                                            and gestures

_____ Proxemics   E. deals with space and how we
                                            use it

_____ Environmental factors   F. deals with physical
                                            surroundings and how the
                                            physical surroundings affect
                                            perceptions of the individual

The presentation has helped me better understand nonverbal communication and
how it exists within society.

_____ strongly agree

_____ agree

_____ neutral

_____ disagree

_____ strong disagree

Chapter Seventeen

Comparing the Role of the Teacher in Small Liberal Arts Colleges and Large Public Universities

This chapter will describe the role transition I experienced when I moved to a small liberal arts college after spending five years at a large research university (and the prior five years at two other state universities). Such considerations will include the effects of size, community, cohesiveness, curricular continuity, financial constraints, quality of academic life, collegiality, proximity, religious mission, and related concerns. Awareness gained from this inquiry provides understanding of how institution size and mission affects the role of the teacher.

A brief chronological review of my academic training and experience will provide insight into the foundation of my perspective. I graduated from a small liberal arts college (Capital University) in Columbus, Ohio, completed my Master's at the State University of New York at Plattsburgh, and earned a Ph.D. from Ohio University. After leaving Ohio University, where I taught four years (three years as a graduate teaching associate), I spent one year as a visiting assistant professor at Miami University in Oxford, Ohio, and then spent five years as an assistant professor at the University of Cincinnati. A combination of personal and professional reasons resulted in my relocating to Columbus, Ohio (my hometown) and accepting a position at Ohio Dominican College.

Ohio Dominican College is a small liberal arts college (roughly 2,100 students) operated by the Dominican Sisters of the Catholic Church. The mission statement of the college is based on the Dominican motto: "to contemplate truth and to share with others the fruits of this contemplation." The common core curriculum requires all students to complete two basic courses in the humanities and two additional "thematics courses" that deal with topics related to the humanities subject area.

The University of Cincinnati is a large comprehensive research university (roughly 36,000 students attend the main and branch campuses). The main campus is second in size in Ohio only to Ohio State University. The University of Cincinnati is owned and operated by the state of Ohio and is comprised of eleven separate colleges (each has individual curriculum requirements). The transition from large research university to small liberal arts college was made easier because I had attended a small liberal arts college as an undergraduate. Discussion of differences between the large research university and small liberal arts college environments will focus on three primary areas: institution size, institution focus, and institution ownership. These three areas are interrelated and affect the role of the teacher.

Institution size is the most concrete area. The physical size of the large university and proportionate number of students, faculty, administrators, and staff evidences a striking contrast with the small liberal arts college.

This factor creates a number of subfactors that affect the role of the teacher. I came to a department comprised of two full-time faculty from a department comprised of eighteen full-time faculty. Thus, discussions about curriculum and classroom procedures occur much easier with the smaller department.

The smaller student body provides a framework for a more cohesive college community. Students know each other and the faculty. The sense of familiarity benefits the classroom and the social atmosphere of the campus. Classroom cohesiveness rarely needs to be built, as it can generally be assumed. This enhances student responsibility for their behavior (attendance, participation, quality of work, and dedication to group membership during group assignments). Similarly, ethical concerns receive more attention because of the size (and resulting familiarity) and the religious nature of the college.

Proximity, as a consideration, is commensurate with student body size. Classes at Ohio Dominican College are taught primarily in three main buildings (one of which houses the main administrative offices and dining hall). This perpetuates considerable interaction (in and out of the classroom) among students with different academic majors. Thus, the smaller (but diverse) student body means a typical classroom will be comprised of students with varied backgrounds and academic interests. The heterogeneity of such a classroom does not suffer from homogeneous familiarity, or "academic blindspots," frequently found in classes comprised of students majoring in the same subject area.

A benefit of teaching at a smaller institution (for me) is being able to consistently teach in the same classroom. This generally leads to faculty members taking ownership for the classrooms in which they teach. Classrooms are rarely littered and vandalism is rare. When I taught at the University of Cincinnati, furniture in some classrooms had to be chained to the wall to discourage theft.

One might think a small college population would lack diversity. The extent of academic diversity is limited compared to large research universities (because of faculty size) but student body ethnic and racial diversity is similar to that of larger universities. The percentage of minority and international students parallels that of Ohio State University, which boasts more than 50,000 students. Fortunately, the aforementioned variables of cohesiveness, size, proximity, and familiarity create an environment that encourages open exchange of ideas among culturally different students in the classroom. Cross-cultural relations are far less strained than what the author experienced at larger universities. Thus, teaching style can build on this cross-cultural appreciation.

The *Chronicle of Higher Education* carries periodic reports about the increase of race-related violence on university campuses in the United States. The following is a purely subjective observation but it can be used as an indicator. During my years of teaching at Ohio Dominican College I have never known of an act of violence at the college that was racially motivated, nor have I ever heard a racial slur directed to or about anyone. This cross-cultural tolerance allows for more genuine classroom discussion regarding cross-cultural differences.

Institution focus is affected by a number of variables. The mission statement of the institution can be such a variable. I have been a faculty member at three large state universities. I never saw an emphasis on university mission statements (if they existed) at these institutions. Ohio Dominican College frequently refers to its mission statement in its literature and the mission statement is clearly recognized as a referent in curriculum development and campus governance.

Related to the Ohio Dominican mission statement is its emphasis on the humanities. As noted earlier, all students take two basic courses in the humanities curriculum. These two courses trace the development of western civilization from the Greeks to present. The humanities faculty is comprised of faculty from various academic departments within the college. Since all students take these courses, faculty can prepare lectures with the assurance students have studied (or are currently studying) primary individuals who have affected the development of western thought. This factor is enhanced because the humanities faculty is relatively small and there is considerable continuity among curricular objectives stressed. This continuity is paralleled in the common core course requirements all students must complete.

Curricular continuity at the University of Cincinnati is far more difficult because of the size of the institution. The university is comprised of eleven separate colleges, each with it's own curricular emphasis. The colleges are linked (students can take courses outside the college of the major) but each college has a considerable degree of autonomy.

Institutional focus is also affected strongly by the religious orientation of Ohio Dominican College. Meetings frequently begin with prayer and some classes begin with prayer. Student organizations and the campus atmosphere reflect a Catholic emphasis. Artwork and artifacts clearly evidence Christian beliefs (i.e., some classrooms have crucifixes above the chalkboards). Religious emphasis in public universities is rare. I speculate such emphasis is rare because of the separation of church and state.

Ohio Dominican College is supported primarily through tuition dollars. This affects the organizational culture as we are all aware we cannot afford to be wasteful. Unproductive employees are rare. My experience in the state system exposed me to a more liberal fiscal approach. State universities are supported primarily by the state. As with any public bureaucracy, unproductive employees and unproductive programs can be more easily sheltered from scrutiny. In private colleges, wasted financial resources equates to, among other things, smaller financial reserves, which equates to smaller salary increases. Waste affects all employees.

There are negative factors that indirectly affect teaching style when one moves from a large research university to a small liberal arts college. Such factors generally include smaller salaries and fewer benefits for faculty, less academic diversity among faculty (due to smaller size), and less monetary support for research and convention travel. One often hears nobody enters a career in education to get rich. This is especially true in the private college sector. The *Chronicle of Higher Education* periodically publishes data that substantiates this perspective. The sense of purpose and quality of life index can counter-balance this lack of economic remuneration, however.

Another consideration affecting institutional focus is the concern with teaching and research. Smaller colleges generally are more concerned with quality teaching and less concerned with research. Subsequently there is less expectation of faculty research. Large public universities generally value research over teaching. Subsequently there is greater expectation of faculty research.

Institution ownership is the third area that was highlighted earlier as a primary category for consideration. Institution ownership, in this case, deals with how faculty relate to the institution, rather than who literally "owns" the physical property. I have seen examples of faculty ownership at private colleges and public universities but feel faculty ownership is much stronger in private colleges.

Public universities are more likely to have unionized faculties. Thus, rights and responsibilities are directly outlined. Private colleges are less likely to have unionized faculties. Secondary responsibilities are generally implied. Faculty are motivated more by "good will" (good of the order) than by "legal" responsibilities. Unions obviously have strong points but often inhibit trust and genuine concern.

As one of two members of the communication arts faculty, I teach a wide range of courses in the communication arts curriculum. I taught far fewer courses while teaching in the state system. I was more of a "specialist" in fewer areas than a generalist in many areas. As a faculty member at a small college I am less inclined to avoid tasks that are not in my job description.

A result of this type of ownership in the small college is that the faculty member is less an "affiliate" of the institution. He or she is the institution. The faculty member in the large public institution can be more of an academic subcontractor, whereas the small college faculty member can be more of an all-around role model. I have a picture of each class I have taught at Ohio Dominican.

An overall benefit of the small college is the stronger sense of community. During my years in the state system I never met a university president. I don't fault the universities for this. Institution size simply does not promote such interaction. At Ohio Dominican, however, faculty and staff informally eat lunch with the president and other administrators on a regular basis.

Senior administrators in large public universities can seem distant and out of touch with faculty concerns. Again, institution size almost guarantees this situation. However, informally eating together and similar informal activities in small colleges help perpetuate a "trickle down" of trust. One evening a university president spent a night in a dormitory to evidence his empathy and understanding with students. There was an upbeat story about it in the newspaper the following day. The president of Ohio Dominican is a Dominican sister. She *lives* in a dormitory room year round.

This chapter is not intended to be a conclusive "last word" on the comparison between small liberal arts colleges and large public universities. I intend this to be one person's perspective on how institution size, institutional focus, and institutional ownership affect the role of the teacher. My interaction with colleagues from both types of institutions support the positions stated but there are obviously exceptions. Still, even in general terms, the aforementioned effects are thought provoking.

Conclusion

The Personal Effects of Participant Observation
on the Participant Observer

This chapter will focus on participant observation, a particular approach within qualitative research, and the effect it can have on the self-concept of the participant observer. Participant observation allows for what Howard S. Becker underlines as "rich experiential context of observation of the event and observation of previous and following events" (Filstead 1970, 141). Participant observation has been used widely in the past and has been applied in a variety of contemporary research settings.

In "A Naturalistic Study of the Meanings of Touch," Jones and Yarbrough (1985) used participant observation to examine the meanings-in-context of touching reported by persons from their daily interactions. Similarly, Owen (1984) used participant observation to study teacher classroom management communication. Gerry Philipsen used participant observation in "Speaking 'Like a Man' in Teamsterville" to find how groups view speaking as an effective means of social influence. He states there is a lack of information in this area and this deficit "should be remedied by descriptive and comparative studies of American speech communities" (Philipsen 1975).

I believe researchers who undertake participant observation studies are likely to experience an altered self-concept as a result of their field experience. The degree of alteration is correlated with the degree of personal involvement.

Review of participant observation studies reveals a tendency of participant observers to describe specific procedures but to provide little discussion of personal experiences.

> Reports about field research usually describe the methods and techniques of the research. Less often do they tell of the researcher's social and emotional experience . . . . These topics are more often discussed in personal conversations between field researchers than written about in the literature. (Shaffir, Stebbins and Turowetz 1980, vii)

I have been surprised at the lack of discussion of personal experiences by participant observers. "What good is a research design that does not include some reference to those who will execute it" (Hughes 1964, 82) or who have executed it?

This chapter will analyze personal effects felt by participant observers, as a result of their research, and discuss the impact of such effects on researcher self-concept. This discussion will include a description of my experiences as a participant observer and the subsequent personal effects I have felt.

A primary form of personal involvement occurs when the distinction between objective observation and subjective participation is not clear. This dilemma is inherent within participant observations. "The outstanding peculiarity of this method is that the observer, in greater or less degree, is caught up in the very web of social interaction which he observes, analyzes, and reports" (Hughes 1960, xiv). There is considerable opportunity for the participant observer to experience conflict between his or her goals as an observer and his or her goals as a participant.

Review of participant observation literature indicates subjects generally respond to participant observers, in the long term, as participants (rather than observers). "Because he is a participant, even if he announces to people that he is there to study them (as I did most of the time in my fieldwork) people soon forget why he is there, and react to him as a participant" (Gans 1968, 305).

A variety of participant observers who have studied various social phenomena indicate a transition and conflict between their observer and participant roles. The transition and conflict involves the extremes of being a stranger (observer) and being a friend (participant). Personal effects, and subsequent self-concept alterations, can occur within the participant observer during involvement with the studied phenomena, even though the participant observer may be fully aware of his or her observation and participation goals. Mere exposure can manipulate, positively or negatively, the frame of reference of the participant observer.

Blanche Geer explains changes that were felt after three days of fieldwork in a college environment.

> Before entering the field, I thought of them as irresponsible children. But as I listened to their voices, learned their language, witnessed gesture and expression, and accumulated the bits of information about them which bring people alive and make their problems real, I achieved a form of empathy with them and became their advocate. (Geer 1967, 394-395)

She reports observers who began work months later experienced the same change, but not until they entered the field. Oddly enough, her actual field notes do not discuss this change.

Barrie Thorne researched the draft resistance movement in Boston during the Vietnam War. Her inner conflict between her goals as a participant and as an observer are apparent within her discussion of her personal experience as a participant observer. "The conflicts I experienced between being a committed participant and an observing sociologist often took the form of great pangs of guilt, and a sense that I was betraying the movement" (Thorne 1979).

Robert Bogdan did fieldwork involving mentally disabled individuals. He explains an instance where the gap between stranger (observer) and friend (participant) was bridged. "When we were told that Pattie wanted to leave the state school but had no place to go, we began looking around for a family that might be willing to provide a place for her to stay. We found a home; it was mine" (Bogdan 1980, 240).

My experience with participant observation occurred during my doctoral dissertation research. Participant observation was my primary method for data collection. The problem of the study dealt with conflict resolution communication attempts practiced by the Woodstock Food Cooperative (see chapter 9). I wanted to find if the ideals of the counterculture were evidenced in the communication attempts at conflict resolution. The co-op presented itself as being based on a countercultural philosophy and was studied as a representative organization of the counterculture.

Results of the study indicated the co-op practiced only superficially a countercultural philosophy. The co-op presented itself as using a consensus process in formal situations, but analysis found it actually used a form of voting. The co-op presented itself as egalitarian in informal situations, but analysis found it actually had a recognized hierarchy among the membership. Thus, the co-op presented itself as practicing a countercultural philosophy, but analysis found it actually practiced dominant culture approaches in communication attempts at conflict resolution.

The hypothesis of the study was not found to be true. I had expected to find that the co-op, as a representative organization within the counterculture, would utilize a consensus process in formal situations and practice egalitarian ideals in informal situations. I was both academically and personally surprised when my data disproved my hypothesis.

As an individual who associated himself with the counterculture and believed the counterculture offered a necessary alternative, I personally hoped there would be stronger distinctions between the counterculture and dominant culture conflict resolution communication attempts. This would have indicated a stronger distinction between the philosophies of the counterculture and dominant culture. The discovery that such strong distinctions do not exist affected my evaluation of one of my primary groups and in turn affected my self-concept.

Prior to the study, I had been involved with a variety of organizations within the counterculture for roughly three years. I associated myself with the counterculture very strongly during those years, both in thought and appearance. This interest with the counterculture stemmed, in part, from my experience as a second lieutenant in the Air Force.

I was enrolled in ROTC as an undergraduate student and entered the Air Force six months after graduation. After a year in the service, I applied for (and was granted) an early release from active duty. The release was under honorable conditions and was sanctioned through an Air Force program that allowed officers to return to graduate school, but still maintain their position in the inactive reserve. I have since reentered the active reserve.

My countercultural leanings were in response to the impersonal bureaucracy that I experienced while in the Air Force. I did not experience serious disagreement with the goals of the military, rather, I experienced Roszak's explanation of the counterculture. Roszak explains counterculture as arising from a youthful revulsion at technocracy. It represents a refusal to surrender spontaneity to artificiality. The counterculture serves to reassert life and joy in the face of impersonal organization (Roszak 1969, 2).

During the early months of the study, I concentrated on achieving as high a degree of objectivity as possible. I did not want my personal countercultural learnings to influence my academic observations. I wanted the data to speak for itself and it did. My data (from observations, interviews, surveys, and review of literature written by or about the organization) indicated the countercultural base of the co-op, and related organizations, was much more superficial than anticipated. The superficial trends were consistently evident from the start of the study.

The consistencies in the data encouraged me academically, but discouraged me personally. I initially questioned the sincerity of the counterculture and then began to question my future personal involvement with the counterculture. Could I better achieve my altruistic aims through a different means? I had originally identified strongly with the co-op membership, and related organizations, but my personal orientation shifted away from this identification during the study. The shift was evidenced in my personal journal.

> My views have changed since I started the study. The distinctions between dominant culture organizations and countercultural organizations seem to be superficial. I think I can promote more (realistic) social change by working within the system than by working outside of it. Some may call it "selling out." I'll call it disillusionment. The goals are still the same . . . I think I'll just try another path for a while. (Field notes 1982)

This personal questioning occurred, little by little, during the course of the data-gathering period, rather than through an abrupt realization.

Rosalie Wax shares a similar experience in "Final Thoughts: How Fieldwork Changed Me." "What changed me irrevocably and beyond repair were the things I learned . . . these irrevocable changes involved replacing mythical and ideological assumptions with the correct (though often painful) facts of the situation" (Wax 1971). As with Wax, what changed me irrevocably were the things I learned. These changes involved replacing personal ideological assumptions "with the correct (though often painful) facts of the situation."

The strongest irrevocable change occurred near the end of the data-gathering period. I had just finished filing my annual federal income tax forms when I questioned the paradox of working for peace (through the counterculture) while paying for military buildup (through taxes). It was apparent to me that most of my countercultural colleagues, except for the handful of war-tax resisters I knew of, were caught in this contradiction. I could see little rationale in working to counter a system that I was financially supporting. My subsequent direction, since this learning experience, has been to work for change within the system.

Since completing my participant observation study I have reflected on my fieldwork experience a good deal. It was academically rewarding, as a Ph.D. dissertation, and it was equally personally rewarding as a learning experience. My initial motivation in doing research for this article stemmed from an interest in learning about the personal experiences of other participant observers and to see what consistencies, if any, exist among people who have used the participant observation method.

Participant observation has been used by a variety of researchers, in all areas of the social sciences, to investigate a wide diversity of research problems. It is difficult to speculate on the psychological make-up of participant observers. A common thread that does exist within most participant observation accounts is the concern with objectivity—not necessarily achieving total objectivity, but consistently working to maintain a high degree of it. This would require a particular ability to detach oneself periodically from one's personal frame of reference. "It is doubtful whether one can become a good social reporter unless he has been able to look, in a reporting mood, at the social world in which he was reared" (Hughes 1960, xi).

As a participant observer who associated himself with the counterculture, and who has done fieldwork within the counterculture, I am particularly interested in Herbert Gans' discussion of fieldworkers.

> My hunch is that fieldwork attracts a person who, in Everett Hughes' words, "is alienated from his own background," who is not entirely comfortable in his new

roles, or who is otherwise detached from his own society; the individual who is more comfortable as an observer than as a participant. (Gans 1968, 317)

The alienation emphasized by Hughes parallels the alienation frequently felt within the counterculture (Roszak 1969, 2).

I believe concern with the personal effects of a method, in this case participant observation, is central to understanding the entire research process. "What good is a research design that does not include some reference to those who will execute it" (Hughes 1964, 82) or who have executed it? My review of the literature reveals a minimal fund of information regarding the personal effects of such research. This report is intended as a contribution to the fund.

References

Bogdan R. 1980. "Interviewing People Labeled Retarded," in W.B. Shaffir, R.A. Stebbins, and A. Turowetz, eds., *Fieldwork Experience: Qualitative Approaches to Social Research*. New York: St. Martin's Press

Field notes, February 5, 1982. Reflections on my personal involvement as a participant observer.

Filstead, W. 1970. *Qualitative Methodology*. Chicago: Markham Publishing Co.

Gans, H.J. 1968. "The Participant Observer as a Human Being: Observations on the Personal Aspects of Fieldwork," in H.S. Becker, B. Geer, D. Riesman, and R.S. Weiss, eds., *Institutions and the Person*. Chicago: Aldine Publishing, Co.

Geer, B. 1967. "First Days in the Field," in P.E. Hammond, ed. *Sociologists at Work*. Garden City, NY: Doubleday and Co.

Hughes, E.C. 1964. "French Canada: The Natural History of a Research Project," in A.J. Vidick, J. Bensman, and M.R. Stein. *Reflections of Community Studies*. New Wiley and Sons.

Hughes, E.C. 1960. "Introduction," in B.H. Junker, *Fieldwork*. Chicago: University of Chicago Press.

Jones, S.E. and Yarbrough, A.E. 1985. "A Naturalistic Study of the Meanings of Touch," *Communication Monographs* 52, 19-56.

Owen, W.F. 1984. "Teacher Classroom Management Communication: A Qualitative Case Study," *Communication Education* 33, 137-142.

Philipsen, G. 1975. "Speaking 'Like a Man' in Teamsterville: Culture Patterns of Role Enactment in an Urban Neighborhood," *Quarterly Journal of Speech* 61, 22.

Roszak, T. 1969. *The Making of a Counterculture*. Garden City, NY: Anchor Books.

Shaffir, W.B., Stebbins, R.A. and Turowetz, A. 1980. *Fieldwork Experience: Qualitative Approaches to Social Research*. New York: St. Martins Press.

Thorne, B. 1979. "Political Activist as Participant Observer: Conflicts of Commitment in a Study of the Draft Resistance Movement of the 1960s," *Symbolic Interaction* 2, 83.

Wax, R. 1971. *Doing Fieldwork: Warnings and Advice*. Chicago: University of Chicago Press.

Index

occulesics, 127
Office of Social Actions, 9-11
organizational culture, 131

participant observation, 75-76, 82-85
    167-172
pedodontic dentistry, 125-128
Perot, Ross, 109-112
prejudice, 11
proximics, 48, 128
proximity, 162
psychological need theory, 87
Public Affairs Video Archives, 109-110
public speaking, 141-152

qualitative research, 167

Reich, Steven, 113, 115
reliability, 85-87
Roszak, Theodore, 113, 170
Rwanda, 28, 32

Senegal, 43
Shalikashvili, General John, 37
Somalia, 28-29, 32

South African Universities, 13-19
Steele, Shelby, 64
subliminal communication, 141-152
symbolic interactionism, 75, 77-82

tactilics, 127-128
Taiwan sovereignty, 51-59
teacher's role, 161-165
Triandis, Harry, 64

Uniform Code of Military Justice, 10
United Nations, 29
U.S. Air Force, 9-12
U.S. National Security Strategy,
    27-38

validity, 85-87
vocalics, 48

Wax, Rosalie, 171

Xinhua News Agency, 52

Yugoslavia, 28, 36

Zhao, Ziyang, 53

About the Author

Jim Schnell is a Professor of Communication Studies at Ohio Dominican College in Columbus, Ohio. He completed his Ph.D. at Ohio University in 1982 and has authored four books, more than forty book chapters and journal articles, and more than one hundred conference presentations dealing with interpersonal and cross-cultural communication. He has been to China ten times and taught as a visiting professor at Northern Jiaotong University in Beijing, China. Schnell is a Lieutenant Colonel in the U.S. Air Force (Reserve), where he is an Assistant Air Attaché to China.